D1410877

English ⌗ Heritage
Book of
Ironbridge Gorge

English Heritage
Book of
Ironbridge Gorge

Catherine Clark

B.T. Batsford Ltd/English Heritage
London

© Catherine Clark 1993

First published 1993

All rights reserved. No part of this publication
may be reproduced, in any form or by any
means, without permission from the Publisher

Typeset by Lasertext Ltd, Stretford,
Manchester
and printed in Great Britain by
The Bath Press, Bath

Published by B T Batsford Ltd
4 Fitzhardinge Street, London W1H 0AH

A CIP catalogue record for this book is
available from the British Library

ISBN 0 7134 6737 1 (cased)
0 7134 6738 X (limp)

Contents

Illustrations

Colour plates

Acknowledgements

The archaeological information on which this book is based derives from several sources; primarily the work of the Ironbridge Gorge Museum Trust Archaeology Unit (1981-9) under the direction of John Malam, David Higgins, myself, Rafael Isserlin and Michael Trueman, assisted by many workers too numerous to thank individually. It also calls upon the results of the Nuffield Archaeological Survey of the Ironbridge Gorge, undertaken with Judith Alfrey between 1985 and 1987, and funded by the Nuffield Foundation. Historical aspects of the study have relied upon the work of Dr Barrie Trinder and also G.C. Baugh, who generously made available the text of the forthcoming Volume 10 of the *Victoria County History of Shropshire*. The maps and reconstructions have been prepared by Judith Dobie of English Heritage.

The staff of the Ironbridge Gorge Museum offered much useful criticism, and in particular I would like to thank Stuart Smith, David de Haan and Michael Vanns for making available their own research. Many of the illustrations were based on work compiled for the model housed in the Museum of the River, and others come from the index of images held by the museum library. The library staff, Marilyn Higson and John Powell, helped in locating photographs and answered endless awkward questions.

Many others have provided support and assistance including Ivor Brown, Ruth Denison, Paul Drury, Lord and Lady Forester, Katie Foster, Tom Foxall, Melanie Heywood, Mark Horton, Stephen Johnson, Peggy Lyon, Ron Miles, Nicola Smith, Joanne Smith, Paul Stamper, Michael Stratton, Sarah Vernon-Hunt, Shelley White, Michael Worthington and my nanny Gillian Sykes, without whom life would have been impossible. Finally, I would like to dedicate this book to Stuart Smith in acknowledgement of his contribution to the Museum and to my parents, whose faith in me has not always been justified.

Illustrations and photographs have been individually acknowledged, and numbers in figure captions refer to the IGMT Documentation system or Shropshire Record Office numbers (SRO). **Colour plate 3** is reproduced by kind permission of Sir Alexander Gibb & Partners. **Colour plate 4** by permission of the Science Museum and **59** with the permission of the Trustees of the Victoria and Albert Museum.

Introduction

The Iron Bridge is one of the most famous monuments of the Industrial Revolution. A graceful arc of cast iron, crossing the river Severn in Shropshire, it was the first major bridge in the world to be built of cast iron. Five roughly semi-circular ribs support a deck with iron rails, and a delicately cast centrepiece, with the motto 'erected in 1779' cast into it. On one of the ribs is cast 'THIS BRIDGE WAS CAST AT COALBROOK DALE AND ERECTED IN THE YEAR MDCCLXXIX'. Two further rows of ribs, iron uprights and a circle fill the space between the bridge and the stone piers from which it springs. To the north is a solid stone abutment, to the north two stone piers with a smaller iron arch between them. The overall impression is one of delicacy and strength, as the arch rises over the river between the towering hills on either side (1).

The bridge represents many things – when it was first built, it was actively promoted in order to publicize the possibilities of new forms of cast iron as well as the abilities of the ironmasters of Coalbrookdale as the area was then known. The bridge became so well known that it gave its name to the settlement of Ironbridge which grew up after the construction of the bridge, and the name is now used to refer to the whole area. Today as a focus for the attention of at least 800,000 tourists a year, and long after cast iron ceased being used in bridge building, the bridge remains an extraordinary monument, representing the triumph of ingenuity over natural obstacles and the achievements of the Industrial Revolution.

Standing on the Iron Bridge and looking down the river, or up to the hills on the south side, the striking impression of the Gorge is one of greenery. The whole of the south bank is wooded, and beyond Ironbridge, the trees on either side begin to close towards each other, creating a green tunnel. From the same viewpoint may be seen the town of Ironbridge stretching across the northern bank, the clusters of houses at the foot of the Iron Bridge on the south bank, and amongst the woods downstream are the settlements of Coalport and Jackfield. This is not what one might expect to see in an area which was once the hub of the Industrial Revolution, the site of flaming furnaces and driving engines.

Scattered amongst this greenery are the remains of industries – old furnaces, brickworks, coal-mines, railways, the scars of limestone working. Examined more closely, many of the houses which survive today are those of the industrial workforce, and most of the other buildings have industrial origins. It is a landscape neither urban nor rural; it does not fit neatly into any of the traditional prescribed categories.

This landscape has been the setting for many famous historical events and innovations, but it is the construction of the Iron Bridge which is perhaps the best known. The building of the bridge demonstrated to the world the properties of cast iron, produced from coke to a new method, that was to have a profound influence on the way in which iron was manufactured and used in building and machinery, and thus upon the course of the Industrial Revolution. Coalbrookdale was also the place where, seventy years earlier, the grandfather of the builder of the Iron Bridge, Abraham Darby I had experimented with the production of iron using coke, rather than charcoal. These experiments had been undertaken at an old iron furnace at Coalbrookdale, about 1km (0.6 miles)

1 *Aerial view of the Iron Bridge at the beginning of this century. Today the landscape is less bare and many of the buildings around either end of the bridge have been demolished* (IGMT 1984.4344).

to the north of the Iron Bridge. The implication of this discovery was that the making of iron was freed from the dependence upon charcoal, and thus upon dwindling supplies of wood. Coal was available and plentiful, and the use of coal in smelting enabled ironmaking to take place on a very much larger scale.

The Iron Bridge and Abraham Darby's furnace at Coalbrookdale are perhaps the best known surviving monuments from this era. Yet within the Gorge there are very many more sites of industrial importance. Several, including Bedlam and Blists Hill Furnaces, the encaustic tileworks at Jackfield and the Hay Inclined Plane have been preserved within the setting of the Ironbridge Gorge Museum, but many more survive, scattered about the landscape. Some are in back yards or on private land, and are not publicly accessible; others lie in the woodlands and can be explored on foot. Taken together, these sites represent an extraordinary richness of industrial remains, concentrated in a small area.

It is clear from these remains that the Iron Bridge was not built in a vacuum, but in a busy valley full of mines and industries, railways and cottages. In order to understand how and why the bridge was built, it is necessary to look more closely at the landscape around it. What was there before the bridge? How did it influence the siting and construction of the bridge? Why was a bridge needed? What happened after the bridge was built? Answers to some of these questions can be found in the landscape.

This book is intended to be an introduction to reading this landscape and to beginning to understand what it can tell us about the past. It is not a full history of the Gorge; a more detailed treatment may be found elsewhere. This book sets out to place the Iron Bridge firmly in its setting, and to explore the surviving industrial remains in the landscape from an archaeological perspective.

What can archaeology contribute to an understanding of the events of the past few hundred years, given the amount of surviving documentary evidence? Archaeology is a notoriously expensive occupation, which can rarely provide precise dates or the names of individuals, and perhaps the time might be better spent in the record office. And, what is the point in excavating the remains of relatively modern industries?

This view ignores the reality of archaeology today. Collecting archaeological evidence is not just a matter of using an excavator's trowel; archaeologists would regard their evidence as covering everything from standing buildings to buried sites, medieval fields to concrete bridges. Physical evidence is, for the archaeologist, the primary source of information.

Documentary evidence inevitably does not cover all the elements we wish to explain – sites we can see which are not documented, changes to buildings which cannot be explained and whole industries for which there is archaeological but not documentary evidence. The survival of documents is a random matter, and even in a well researched area like the Gorge there are vast gaps in the coverage.

But archaeology can do more than just fill in the gaps in the documents. It is possible to see not what people boasted about in their letters, but what they did. The make-do-and-mend approach of many industrialists becomes very evident as one looks at the sites cobbled out of earlier buildings. The degree of conservatism that operated over hundreds of years is apparent in almost every industry. We can see investment and capital assets in buildings;

decay and abandonment in the remains of sites (2). It is possible to infer social aspirations from people's possessions, their houses and where they were built. Attitudes to land, minerals, neighbours and industry can all be seen. It is different evidence, but no less valuable.

Of course there are problems with the archaeological evidence – it is not possible to see individuals, nor politics, prices or markets. National statistics so beloved by economic historians are almost impossible to compile from archaeological data, as are many aspects of conventional social history relating to people, their attitudes and beliefs. The error margin on archaeological dating techniques is often too high to make absolute archaeological dates of any use in industrial archaeology.

Nevertheless, archaeological evidence does have strengths if treated carefully. Like the

2 *Removal of a boiler from the Blists Hill Ironworks, 1918. Disused industrial sites were usually cleared of all equipment, scrap metal and even building materials, leaving surprisingly little for the modern archaeologist (IGMT 1986.14022).*

historian, the archaeologist has to take a critical approach to data which is often partial and biased; as the historian looks at the context of a document, so the archaeologist must look carefully at the context of the field data. For this, archaeologists have developed a number of field techniques. Most of these derive from excavation, but they can also be used to understand landscapes and standing buildings.

The two principal ideas which underpin this critical approach to archaeological data are *time* and *space*. The archaeologist sets any observation in its temporal and spatial context in order to understand it. It is not possible to understand a building, for example, unless we can see the pattern of how it has changed through time. Equally, the setting of that building is important in order to reconstruct why it was built.

This study, then, is an attempt to set the Iron Bridge in its archaeological context of time and space. It begins by travelling back in time to the medieval setting of the Gorge, and moves through to the present day, while at the same time considering the broad spatial issues of what the Gorge looked like, how it was shaped and what problems it created for the early industrialist.

The Iron Bridge is a magnificent monument, to be admired however often one passes it, but it is not a bridge built in isolation. The achievement of the bridge is mirrored in the great sloping sides of the Gorge, the fast flowing river and the fickle geological strata which have defeated many other bridge builders. It is an integral and inseparable part of the industrial landscape in which it was set.

1

Medieval origins

In 1708 when Abraham Darby I came to the Gorge, he found an already busy, industrialized landscape. There were coal-mines dug hundreds of yards into the hillside, small-scale ironworks including a charcoal blast furnace and perhaps a steelworks, some early pottery manufacture and several mills. Some of the earliest wooden waggonways or railways in Britain were in use to transport coal down to boats on the riverside. There were new settlements of industrial workers in Broseley and Madeley in little brick cottages, and the economy was already moving away from the traditional manorial agriculture.

The landscape which Darby found had its roots in the medieval period when much – but not all – of the Gorge fell under the control of the great Priory of Much Wenlock (3). During this period a framework of landholding and control was established, the three parishes of Broseley, Madeley and Benthall with their medieval centres developed, and the disposition of woods and waste, commons and fields laid down. This pattern did not become fossilized, but it did provide a broad structure for the development of land, reminders of which can be seen today.

The earliest settlements

In south Shropshire, ancient woodland survived to a very late date. Apart from a bronze axe, found in the river Severn, there is little evidence for any prehistoric activity in this area, and the nearest Roman settlements lie to the south-west at Wroxeter, or to the north at Red Hill in what is now Telford.

The earliest settlements date to the seventh century AD, and consisted of small clearings in the woodlands. Saxon charters mention land-holdings high on the hill above the Gorge at Madeley, and on the south bank at Caughley. It is worth noting that these – and many other – place names bear the suffix '-ley' ('-leg', '-lea'), often taken to indicate woodland clearing. The only archaeological evidence for early settlement is the late Saxon church at Barrow to the south, which suggests a substantial population in this area during the pre-Conquest period. The Caughley settlement contracted, but the Madeley settlement may well lie under or near the centre of Madeley today.

Monastic control

In 727, the lands at Madeley and Caughley were sold to Milburga, daughter of a sub-king of Mercia who controlled parts of the West Midlands. Milburga was abbess of a double monastery for women and men at Much Wenlock just before 690. The site lies about 6km ($3\frac{3}{4}$ miles) to the south-west of the Gorge, but nothing remains above ground of the original foundation.

The acquisition of land around the Gorge was part of the monastery's developing landholding, which was eventually to encompass both sides of the Gorge, as well as a considerable amount of land to the south. This hold that Wenlock had over the Gorge was to be an important influence on the area during the medieval period, and in fact the pattern of administrative control remained in place until 1966, when Much Wenlock finally ceased to be the centre of district administration.

Most of the buildings that can be seen today at Wenlock Priory post-date its re-founding in 1086 by Roger, Earl of Shrewsbury (4). A new church was built, and the priory buildings laid out to include an elegant chapter house, and a

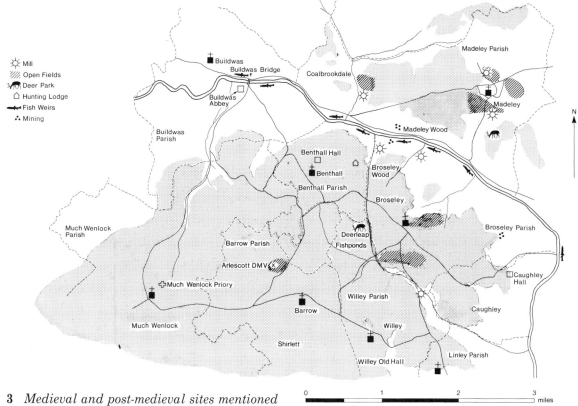

Legend:
- ☼ Mill
- ▨ Open Fields
- 🌲 Deer Park
- ⌂ Hunting Lodge
- ⤜ Fish Weirs
- ∴ Mining

3 *Medieval and post-medieval sites mentioned in the text* (Judith Dobie).

4 *Much Wenlock Priory, looking south-east across the nave* (Michael Worthington).

cloister with a famous stone-carved lavatorium. The Prior's Lodging remains occupied today, and is regarded as one of the finest medieval houses still in occupation in Britain. Recent excavations there have provided evidence for the small-scale industry associated with the refurbishment of the church. There were bowl furnaces in which roof lead was melted and evidence for lead-cutting.

The new priory at Wenlock managed to keep most of the pre-Conquest lands and possessions intact. These included the manor of Madeley, with a large area of woodland sufficient for 400 pigs, and the large parish of Wenlock, south of the Severn, with woodland for 300 pigs. As a number of neighbouring places such as Caughley, Barrow, Linley and possibly Broseley, were not listed in the Domesday survey, it is generally assumed that they were included within the greater parish of Wenlock.

Royal forests and woodland

Above all, the Domesday survey shows how heavily wooded the Gorge was. This may have been one reason for the designation of the whole of the area as the Royal Forests of

Wrekin and Shirlett, soon after the Conquest. Royal Forests were the preserve of the king, who used them for hunting. They were not always wooded, but they did fall under Forest Law, which severely restricted activities such as settlement, clearing, digging or cutting timber. There were fines for those who infringed the king's domain. Given the importance of woodland, and the dominance of woodland in the area, Forest Law may have been a check on economic activity.

The land within the forest was actually held by Wenlock Priory, and even the monks were restricted in the way they could develop their lands. They were fined for 'assarting' or clearing land at Benthall in 1125 and again in Broseley in 1250. Increasingly in the thirteenth and fourteenth centuries, clearances were made by the monks' tenants. Many of the area's outlying farms were established in this way, such as Upper and Lower Riddings, east of Broseley village.

Although hunting was normally reserved for the king, the monks were able to obtain royal sanction for hays or parks at Willey, Deerleap and Madeley. A park was in effect a corral, or area for keeping deer, valued for their meat as well as for sport. Hunting remained important long after this period, and there are two surviving seventeenth-century hunting lodges at Benthall and at Madeley Wood.

In this way, the process of clearing the forests began, either illegally, or by royal decree in order to raise money for the exchequer. The process was accelerated after 'disafforestation', a series of decrees which released the area from Forest Law in the thirteenth and early fourteenth centuries. This meant that land owners and tenants could begin to clear land and to build on it, settlements expanded and new areas were opened.

Nevertheless, woodland remained an important part of the local industrial economy. Field names show that it persisted in Benthall parish, and Madeley and Broseley both had large areas of woodland well into the eighteenth century. There is a clear distinction between the two economically important types of wood – timber, from mature trees including oak, and the smaller coppice wood (5) (usually hazel, oak, beech, ash and hornbeam), used for charcoal burning and for manufacturing items such as hurdles or handles. Timber was used in building, and can be seen in some of the

5 *Cutting coppice wood. Woodland was carefully managed as a valuable economic resource* (Judith Dobie).

earliest structures in the Gorge; it was also in demand by the navy who complained about its scarcity in the seventeenth century. A huge number of oaks was consumed in lime kilns before the use of coal as fuel for burning lime.

One large consumer of timber, especially in the seventeenth century, was mining. When Arthur Young visited Benthall a century later, in 1776, he noted that oak poles were barked and sold as pit props and the bark was sold for tanning. Coppiced poles were used for mine props to support underground galleries and as the rails for wooden railways (see Chapter 8). Equipment for draining mines, such as water channels or barrels and supports for horse gins, carts for transporting coal, all required timber. Miners had to ensure a good supply of timber in order to operate successfully. Supplies of timber from Benthall woods were also linked to the boat-building industry on the south bank of the Gorge at Bower Yard.

'The value of coppice wood is daily declining' wrote another visitor to Benthall in 1803, and by 1844 many of the fields there with woodland names were now arable. Coppicing clearly had been important in the parish, but had subsequently proved uncompetitive. Much of the earlier coppice wood had most likely been burnt for charcoal, on which many early industries – including the iron industry – were dependent.

Medieval settlement

Following disafforestation in the thirteenth century the Priory, under Prior Humbert, gradually began to develop its holdings in the Gorge. It retained a very strong degree of control over its land – it had courts and was able to levy fines. At the death of a tenant, one third of his goods passed in tax to the Priory. Local people complained that it left the population very poor, and was perhaps a disincentive towards cultivating new land.

By this date, there were three distinct settlements in the Gorge, grouped together by the Priory – Broseley and Benthall, both on the south bank, and Madeley on the north. In Broseley the centre of the village was where the church is today. There was a manor house, which has since been lost, a chapel, and a group of houses. Open fields with cultivated strips spread around the town, and there were areas of woodland. The manorial commons were to the north-west, where Broseley Wood is today. New estates had been created in the eastern part of the manor for freeholders.

The medieval centre of Benthall has also disappeared, and all that remain are the faint outlines of a deserted village in the fields behind Benthall Hall. The centre of the village lay here, but had been abandoned by the Civil War, when the Hall was garrisoned. New settlement spread along the roads down to the Gorge, but Benthall never again really developed a proper centre.

In Madeley, the area around the church was the centre of the early medieval settlement and possibly the earlier Saxon one. The present church was rebuilt by Thomas Telford in 1797, but apparently had twelfth-century footings. There were open fields around the town, and woodland down towards the Gorge. Coalbrookdale itself was a small medieval settlement, with an open field system distinct from that of Madeley. A new town was effectively created in Madeley in 1269, when the Priory was granted a market and fair. Long thin burgage plots were laid out along the road to Much Wenlock, with a market place in the centre. The power of the Priory is evident in the order made by the Crown in 1250, to demolish cottages recently built on assarts in the woods, but allowing the Priory to keep its own houses.

This approach to estate management contrasts with that of Buildwas Abbey, a Savignac (and later Cistercian) abbey located just to the west of the Gorge in the fields at the bottom of the Buildwas valley (6). The nave and chancel of the great church survive, together with claustral buildings on the north side, including the chapter house and undercroft. Buildwas was founded in 1135 on land belonging to the Bishop of Chester. Unlike Much Wenlock, it made little attempt to consolidate a local estate, but acquired widely scattered lands in Staffordshire, Derbyshire and Chester. Their local holdings were very modest, and farmed by lay-brothers from the abbey rather than leased out, as were those of Wenlock.

The monks of Buildwas chose a strategic location for their abbey at the junction of a stream (providing water-power) and a river (providing transport). The abbey lay on a route between Much Wenlock and the town of Madeley, where a medieval market had been granted to the Wenlock monks in 1269. However, it was most likely to have been the monks of Buildwas who were responsible for the construction and maintenance of the medieval bridge which formerly existed there (7). Old paintings show it to have had massive cutwaters, pointed arches and pedestrian refuges on the top. The bridge survived until the eighteenth century when it was damaged by floods, repaired, damaged again in the great floods of 1795, and finally replaced by a new bridge in 1795-6.

Medieval industry

Under monastic control there was some industrialization, and in particular, water-powered mills. Because river levels fluctuated dramatically, the Severn was rarely used as a source of power, but the tiny streams which drop down the side valleys to the river could be dammed to provide power. There was a water-mill in the Benthall valley by 1317, another just north of the Blists Hill site on the Washbrook, and two

6 (Above, right) *Buildwas Abbey in 1731, engraved by Samuel and Nathaniel Buck. The ruins were described in 1784 as 'more perfect than most I have seen ... and sweetly situated'* (English Heritage).

7 (Below, right) *The medieval bridge at Buildwas under repair c.1792, painted by Samuel Ireland. The repairs were supervised by Thomas Telford (IGMT SSMT.68).*

THE SOUTH-WEST VIEW OF BILDEWAS-ABBY, IN THE COUNTY OF SALOP.

To Acton Moseley Esqr.
owner of these Remains.
This Prospect is gratefully Inscrib'd by
Yr most Oblig'd Humble Servt
Saml & Nathl Buck.

BILDEWAS or BULDEWAS, was founded & Endow'd by Roger de Clinton Bishop
of Coventry & Litchfield. A.D. 1153. to the honour of St Marys, St Ceaddo or St Chad.)
It had after this, several noble and generous Benefactors, among the Principal were
Walter de Dunstanville & Robert Corbet; which several Benefactions & Estates
were after confirm'd, to them by K. Richard I. An: Reg: I. It's value at the Sup:
pression was 1l.9. 19. 3. ½ Ani. Dug. — 129. 6. 10. Speed. — S.& N. Buck delin et Sculp. 1731.

more in Broseley by 1545. There was probably an early mill in Coalbrookdale as well. Often the dam for a medieval mill was reused again and again by later industries, long after the original installation had disappeared. The dam for the mill which lay to the south of the Iron Bridge may well have been medieval in origin, as may one of the dams for the Coalbrookdale ironworks.

Other traces of medieval enterprise remaining in the landscape are fish weirs (8). These were islands or 'byelets' created in the river to divide the stream. One half was then blocked by a wicker dam in which fish could be caught. Standing by Bedlam Furnaces today, it is possible to see a gravel island which was, in origin, the 'Copie Wear', one of seven fish weirs in Benthall and Broseley. Medieval in origin, during the seventeenth century it was sublet to Thomas Dawley of Benthall, a trowman, at

a cost of 23s 4d. In addition, he was to pay yearly, 'one stick of round eels and one stick of sticke eels' to the landowner. The weir was later known as 'Eaves Mount' (John Eves had owned the land opposite) and several trows ran aground on it.

Building stone and other materials for Buildwas Abbey were quarried in the Gorge. Limestone was brought by road from Benthall Edge and sandstone by river from Broseley. The monks undertook some coal-mining in Broseley and Madeley, and also obtained clay for the decorative floor tiles in the abbey from local clay sources. There was ironstone mining at Little Wenlock, and Wenlock Priory had iron forges in the woods of Shirlett to the south-east. The monks of Buildwas had a small bloomery, producing wrought iron.

The degree of medieval industrialization was not great, however. Unlike areas rich in minerals in other parts of the country, such as the Forest of Dean or the Weald, the early development of mining and ironworking was probably hindered, rather than encouraged, by the monks. Prosperity had declined after a peak in the thirteenth century; the Black Death reduced the population, and settlements such

8 *A fish weir on the river Severn. River traffic could continue to use the barge gutter to the left of the island* (or byelet) *while fish were funnelled into the wicker dam to the right* (Judith Dobie).

as Coalbrookdale seem to have contracted. By 1535 neither abbey was very large – there were only 12 monks at Buildwas and the same number at Wenlock.

The end of monastic control
In 1540 Wenlock Priory was dissolved, and its lands and possessions sold. The Manor of Madeley was bought by Basil Brooke, Speaker of the Commons and a justice, while Benthall passed soon after to Lawrence Benthall. After changing hands several times, the Priory lands in Broseley were acquired by James Clifford in the 1560s, who added them to the other two-thirds of the manor which he had inherited. Land at Willey was acquired by John Weld, a London lawyer. Weld, Benthall, Brooke's grandson and Clifford all set about actively developing the coal and other minerals on their lands, establishing a pattern of industrialization which was to have far reaching effects.

Thus, during the medieval period, a framework of ownership and control was established in the Gorge. Today the differences between one side of the Gorge and the other, between areas of fields, woods and settlement, reflect the landholdings of Wenlock Priory and the medieval land uses which they established. At the Dissolution these landholdings were sold, falling eventually into the hands of several individuals determined to exploit the mineral potential of the land. These individuals, their agents, master colliers and competitors, created a seventeenth-century coal industry of national status, which in turn underpinned the Industrial Revolution of the eighteenth century.

2

Coal – the basis of industrialization

> The business that employs some thousands
> of Men here is the Coal Mines, (for which
> Article only I've seen, Two hundred Sail of
> Vessels lying in and near it)...

It is easy to forget that up to, and in fact during,
the last part of the eighteenth century, the
most important industry in the Gorge was
coal; Benthall and Broseley in 1635 were rated
amongst the main collieries in Britain with a
total output of around 100,000 tons per year.
Without an established coal industry there
would have been no industrial workforce, no
waggonways or wharfs, no fleet of barges, no
raw materials and little of the capital which
was later invested in the iron industry. Coal-
mining was an essential precursor to the
Industrial Revolution in the Gorge.

The expansion of coal-mining was initiated
by a group of entrepreneurs, anxious to develop
the landed estates they had acquired after the
dissolution of the monasteries. They dug mines,
invested in equipment, encouraged new settlers
and created an industrial infrastructure. Coal
in turn attracted the first generation of coal-
using industries in the Gorge such as lead
smelting, tar boiling and pottery making, and
brass manufacture. By the late eighteenth century, coal-mining had become a huge operation
usually linked with ironworking. Money from
coal funded the first ironworks, and soon the
big ironworks began to mine their own coal
as they sought to integrate their activities.
Towards the end of the century, the local coal
industry began to decline as ironmasters turned
to newly-opened seams in the north of the
coalfield, although some mining continued well
after that, usually in conjunction with industries such as brick-making. Opencast mining

still takes place in the area with huge workings
to the north and south of the Gorge.

What can archaeology contribute to the
study of coal-mining? Mines are often dang-
erous or impossible places to enter, and surface
remains such as winding gear have usually been
demolished long ago. But the field evidence for
mining is more varied than that – spoil heaps,
field names, adit entrances, surface collapses
and geological cores all indicate former mines,
while railways, inclines, pumping engines,
wharfs and miners' cottages are all part of the
other activities which mining involved. By
bringing this type of evidence together with
documents, mine plans and other sources, it is
possible to make much better sense of the
contribution of mining to the history of the
landscape.

The exploitation of resources such as coal
was not simply a matter of availability – miners
did not just appear and dig out all the coal
until it was finished. Physical, financial and
even conceptual factors governed the way in
which coal was mined. The basic physical problem was the accessibility of a seam – coal might
remain in the ground if it was too deep to mine
or too difficult to remove the water. In financial
terms, a miner would have to balance the price
the coal might fetch with the cost of mining it.
But mining was also a matter of understanding.
It is possible to trace the changing perceptions
of mine operators as they gradually became
aware of the properties of different seams. At
the same time, industry demanded coal with
increasingly specific properties. By the nineteenth century, the two types of coal recognized
by medieval miners had been divided into ten
or more different seams, which were suitable
for anything from specialist smelting to firing

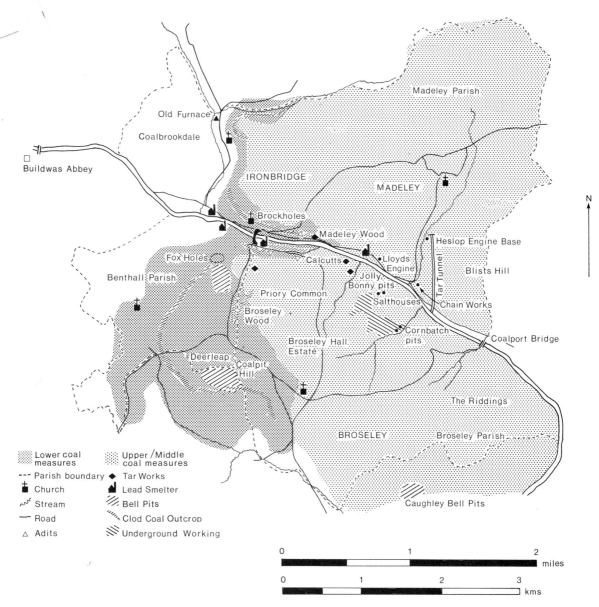

Legend:

- Lower coal measures
- Upper/Middle coal measures
- --- Parish boundary
- ♦ Tar Works
- ✚ Church
- ◢ Lead Smelter
- ∿ Stream
- ⫽ Bell Pits
- — Road
- ⦚ Clod Coal Outcrop
- △ Adits
- ⦚ Underground Working

0   1   2 miles

0   1   2   3 kms

9 *Sites associated with coal-mining. The Lower Coal Measures outcrop to the west and dive deep under the Middle Coal Measures to the east. The coalfield extends north into modern Telford, and a short way to the south towards Linley* (Judith Dobie).

a boiler cheaply. Coal-mining had become a very complex operation.

The different coal seams

In order to understand the evidence in the landscape for mining, it is first necessary to understand the coal beneath the surface. It is important to be aware not only of the many different types of coal, each with distinct properties, but also how easy the coal was to reach. Some seams were easily accessible and worth working, others were too difficult to reach with early technology and were only exploited later.

The river Severn has cut through the Middle and Lower Coal Measures of the Coalbrookdale Coalfield (**10**). These measures contain productive coal seams, interspersed with layers of mudstone, ironstone and clays. Where the river

23

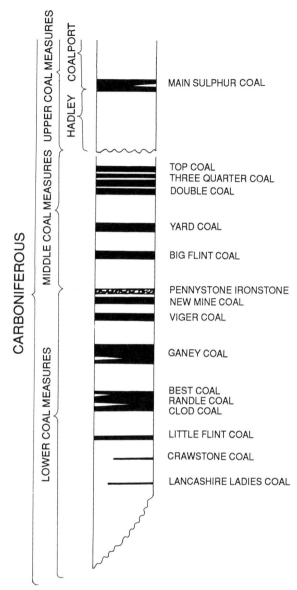

10 *Sequence of coal seams in the Lower and Middle Coal Measures* (Shelley White).

has cut through these seams, they outcrop on the surface and mines can be dug directly into the hillside. To the north-east at Blists Hill, the coal seams are deep and have to be mined through shafts up to 200m (656ft) deep, whereas to the south-west, in Benthall for example, the coal is just below the surface and can be mined in shallow pits or even by open working. The boundary of the Coal Measures to the west is formed by the limestones of Lincoln Hill and

Benthall Edge, while the coal peters out to the east beyond Blists Hill.

Industrialists knew about the quality and occurrence of different seams well before the science of geology was established. Medieval ironsmiths distinguished 'sweet' or 'stinking' coals, today defined as low and high sulphur coals. Sweet coals were suitable for domestic fires, for forging or smithing, while sulphur coals contained too many impurities to be used. Most of the coals in the Gorge – except the Main Sulphur coal – are low in sulphur and would have been suitable for medieval purposes

It is interesting to trace the way in which the variety of coal seams came to be recognized; mining leases often give the names of seams, and quote prices for each type of coal – more for the better seams, less for the poorer ones. For example, the 'Bottom Coal' from Calcutts fetched one shilling per ton in 1659, but all the other coals from the same pit fetched only sixpence per ton. By the 1670s almost every one of the coal seams we know today had been recognized. However, it was with ironworking in the eighteenth century that differences in coal became absolutely critical to the success of industry.

Only one seam was thought to be suitable for iron smelting, Clod Coal. When Abraham Darby came to the Gorge in 1708 and began smelting iron with coke and not charcoal at the old blast furnace in Coalbrookdale, he experimented with different coals. He soon found that only the Clod Coal served his purposes as a result of which Clod Coal became the main coal used in smelting.

So popular was this coal that it is often assumed that the major reason for the ending of iron smelting in the Gorge was that the Clod Coal ran out. In fact the situation is more complex. Coal seams do not always run out – often it simply becomes more expensive to mine the less accessible seams, and easier to get coal from other areas. The working face gets further and further away from the shaft, the mine may be costly to maintain, and closure is inevitable. Some of the old seams are still mined today, because opencast techniques make it economic again. Modern workings at Caughley and Benthall have exposed the old shafts and galleries, and occasionally old tools and equipment.

Changes in iron smelting also meant that the iron industry did not have to rely only on the Clod Coal; new techniques developed in the nineteenth century enabled a greater range of coals could be used. As Parton observed in 1865, there was a great deal of conservatism in the industry:

> The Top, Double Yard and Big Flint coals are good for manufacturing purposes. Occasionally some are coked and used in the furnaces, but the furnace managers, who are often more nice than wise, would rather do without them so long as they can get the famous Clod coal and the Little Flint...Coals which were condemned to all intents and purposes twenty, yea ten years ago, are now being applied successfully.

This quotation shows that the choices industrialists made about the use of resources were not simply based on availability. Ironmasters clearly had preconceived ideas about which coals were suitable for smelting, whatever the experts might tell them.

The earliest mining

Medieval mining certainly took place in the Gorge, but there is little direct field evidence for it. Documentary evidence shows that local coals have been exploited since the thirteenth century, when the monks of Buildwas dug coal at Benthall. In 1235 Philip de Benthall granted the monks right of way over his land for carrying this coal, and in 1326 Adam Peyeson of Buildwas held land at Benthall, with

> quarries of coal of the sea, four labourers to dig the coals, and as many servants as he chose for carrying the coals to the Severn and thence leading them away

At the same time, he was to allow Hugh, Lord of Sheinton enough coal for the lord's own hearth. There are other references to medieval mining; 'coldelfes' in Benthall in 1317, coal-mining at 'Brockholes' in Ironbridge in 1322 and mining in Broseley in 1417-18. Wenlock Priory was involved in mining in its lands in Broseley from at least the sixteenth century, as there were Priory coal pits in 1514 and a 'Coal Meadow' near the High Riddings – a name which means colliery spoil. This mining was scattered, and on a small scale, and has left no discernible traces in the landscape.

The earliest field remains of mining are bell pits and their doughnut-shaped rings of spoil which appear in places where coal seams lie just below the surface (**11**). A bell pit consists

11 *Reconstruction of a bell pit* (Judith Dobie).

of a shaft dug down to the coal seam, with the coal dug from around the base of a shaft. The spoil was thrown up to the surface in a ring around the top of the shaft, resulting in the characteristic pattern of spoil rings. Bell pits required relatively little investment such as pumps or ventilation, and were abandoned once mining became difficult.

An example of a typical small-scale mining area survives at Caughley, to the south-east of Ironbridge. Here is a scatter of 37 bell pits, the line of which follows the outcrop of the Ganey, Best, Randle and Clod Coal seams. Another group to the south had been dug into the Little Flint Coal. These pits clearly demonstrate the preference for some coal seams and not others, and thus it should be possible to predict the occurrence of similar mining remains wherever these seams outcrop on the surface. Field survey does indeed bear this out as bell pits can be found in woods in Benthall at Workhouse Coppice and at Deerleap in Broseley, dug into the Ganey and Best, Randle and Clod seams.

Yet if Benthall was one of the largest collieries in the country, relatively little field evidence survives today to show this. It seems that pits only survive in areas of woodland, but not in fields; here little more than occasional smudges of coal waste can be found in areas where mining might be predicted. Old maps suggest that most of the evidence has been destroyed by the two real threats to early mining remains – modern opencast coal-mining in places where it is perfectly economic to re-open old workings, and modern deep ploughing which has erased the remainder.

The key difficulty with bell pits and other mining evidence is dating it. The Caughley pits cannot be linked to an individual, although we do know that mining was common there in the seventeenth century. But by using stratigraphy, it is possible to show that the pits had been dug away by later mining on the clay outcrop. This clay mining can be linked to a saggar works on the site by 1780, and therefore gives a *terminus ante quem* – a 'time before which' working must have ceased. We can only guess that the bell pits were characteristic of mining in the area up to the early part of the seventeenth century when output reached a peak.

Bell pits were an example of a small-scale mining operation, perhaps undertaken under licence by an individual, and not involving a huge amount of capital. They contrast with the very much larger operations which begin to appear in the seventeenth century.

Entrepreneurs and the seventeenth-century mining boom

Within a century of the Dissolution the Gorge reached national prominence as a source of coal, which became a major strategic resource. The medieval forests and fields were punctuated by shafts and adits, with their horse gins, pumps and winding gear, as well as by roads and some of the first waggonways in the country, leading down to the river. Mining spoil had begun to disfigure the landscape and new industrial settlements had grown up on the old agricul-

tural commons. In 1635 the tiny area of Benthall alone produced 30,000 tons of coal a year, and during the Civil War, the collieries were of such importance that they were seized by Parliamentary forces in order to prevent coal travelling down the Severn to Royalist areas. As a result, there were such shortages in Bridgnorth and Worcester that the townspeople threatened to slay soldiers taking coal to Shrewsbury unless free trade was permitted.

This transformation came about largely through the capital injected into mining by the entrepreneurs, John Weld, James Clifford, Basil Brooke and Lawrence Benthall, who had bought or inherited monastic estates. All were prepared to invest capital in digging mines, building transport links and expanding the mineral potential of their land.

One of the mining techniques which they made use of was the insett or adit which consisted of a tunnel dug straight into the hillside, following the coal seam (**12**). Coal was brought out, and dropped down the hillside into waiting boats, or stacked at wharfs ready to be transported to markets further down the river. Some of these tunnels – such as that at the Lake Head to the west of Bedlam Furnaces – were up to a mile long, and involved extensive engineering in order to keep them in operation. Air shafts were needed for ventilation, extra shafts for access, 'soughs' drained the water, and winding drums and tracks were located at the entrance to drop the coal down to the riverside. Wooden waggonways may also have been used underground for the transport of the coal (**13**).

For all their investment and effort, the coal-mining enterprises of this group of landowners did not necessarily bring long-term prosperity to their families or estates. By the end of the seventeenth century, Broseley had a thriving coal industry, an expanding population and the town was one of the county's largest. Yet in 1613 James Clifford's estates were in debt, in 1630 Weld advised his son to avoid seeking for 'coles' and to invest in land and agriculture and much of Brooke's lands in Madeley were sold off at the end of the century.

These insetts were operated by agents or managers, sometimes on behalf of landowners. For example, in 1608 Jesse Whittingham had the right to all coal and ironstone 'digged within ffower insetts or pitts allreadie begunne by the saied James Clifford'. Whittingham's four insetts can be identified on an early map, situated on the riverside. In 1990 excavation was undertaken to try to locate these insetts, but unfortunately ironstone mining in the nineteenth century had dumped huge quantities of spoil on the riverside which buried any earlier evidence.

A clue to the character and status of these mine managers can be seen from their houses. Another map shows four insetts, at the entrance to three of which is a large house which apparently belongs to the operator of the coal-mine. We know what one of these houses looked like as it survived into this century: a substantial timber-framed building, built in 1654 by Adam Crompton, a ferryman and miner; it was later used as a pub known as the Dog and Duck (14). Adam Crompton was typical of the group of master colliers who played an important role in developing mining, often as managers for landowners.

Coal and settlement

At the other end of the scale were the labourers, or colliers, who dug out the coal for the coal-master. In order to provide labour for the coal-mines, landowners such as James Clifford had encouraged immigrants to settle on the old agricultural commons of the town of Broseley. Local people in the existing agricultural villages were resentful, and described the incomers as

> lewd persons, the Scums and dreggs of many countries from whence they have bine drivern ... theives ... horrible Swearers ... daillie drunkerds, some havinge towe or three wyves a peece now liveing, others...notorious whore mongers

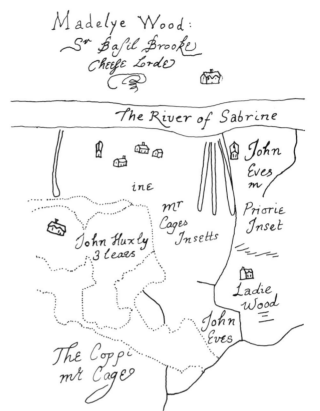

12 *Extract from Samuel Parsons' map of c.1621 showing insetts or horizontal mines extending south from the river* (SRO 1224/Nicola Smith).

13 *Diagram of a coal adit: a long tunnel was dug into the hillside, coal was brought out above the river and let down to waiting boats. This reconstruction is based on a map of c.1676 showing an adit by Adam Crompton's house* (Shelley White).

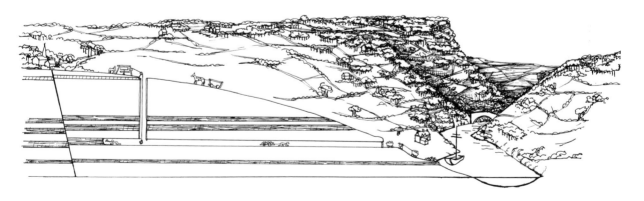

14 *The house of coalmaster Adam Crompton, built in 1654. It was located south-west of the present Free Bridge* (Judith Dobie).

Through these new settlers, coal-mining changed the whole geography of settlement in Broseley parish. By Clifford's death there were settlements on the margin of the old Priory Common, and cottages scattered about Colepitt Hill and in the woodlands down by the river. These were new areas, well away from the traditional agricultural centre of Broseley to the south-east. On the southern section of Priory Common a scattered pattern of settlement grew up, with houses tucked into disorganized plots.

It is amongst this type of settlement in Broseley Wood and on the north bank of the river, that evidence for material possessions culled from probate inventories shows that communities were becoming industrialized. Clocks are increasingly common possessions as people stopped relying on daylight or the seasons to regulate their working patterns. It was becoming less usual for people to own agricultural implements or to keep animals. This suggests that there was less self-sufficiency as people bought food, and gradually moved from an agricultural to an industrial lifestyle.

Little remains of the dwellings of the seventeenth-century miners in this area, but there is evidence for miners' cottages on commons in

the eighteenth century to the north of the Gorge. These were small, often built by miners themselves out of local materials – stone, pieces of mine chain, perhaps thatch on the roof or later tiles. An example of one of these so-called 'Squatter Cottages' has been re-erected at the open-air museum at Blists Hill. It came from the community at Holywell Lane near Lightmoor to the north of the Gorge. The building is of stone, with two rooms; one with a fire served as a kitchen/living area, the other is a bedroom, where the miner, his wife and children (also often employed at the pits) would have slept. A tiny area for storage has been added on to one side.

Most of the similar cottages in the Gorge have long gone, as indeed have many of the original mining settlements at Benthall Marsh, in Mone Wood or in Yates Coppice. Nevertheless, we can assume that there existed an early pattern of scattered mining settlements involving little cottages, in oddly-shaped plots of land on old commons or in woods. Some of the miners had brick cottages built for them by landowners such as Clifford, others may have had to throw up their own dwellings using whatever materials they could find.

It is apparent that by the end of the seventeenth century, the capital injected into mining by the landowners had transformed the settlements of the Gorge. Large, well-equipped mines were capable of producing more coal than the bell pits operated by individual miners. There were roads and railways down to the riverside, and a fleet of boats to transport the coal. There was a new group of mine managers, living fairly prosperous lives in fine houses on the riverside, as well as a whole new population of labourers living in settlements scattered around the valley, set apart from the existing communities, and industrialized in their outlook and way of life.

Most of the coal production had been exported from the Gorge to other coal-using areas; in the early eighteenth century new industries sprang up locally to make use of this resource. It was not just mining but the activities that were linked with mining that paved the way for industrial expansion in the eighteenth century.

Coal and early industries
The most famous of the new coal-using industries was of course Abraham Darby I's success

in using coke to smelt iron at Coalbrookdale. Prior to coming to the area, Darby had been involved in the Bristol brass industry where he had had experience in using coke as a fuel in brass founding, in copper smelting and also in malting. He was thus well aware of the potential of coke.

It has always been assumed that Darby's purpose in coming to the Gorge was to develop the iron industry, but new research has shown that his original intention may have been to set up a brass works, making use of the local coals which he knew to be suitable. Some copper smelting and brass founding were actually undertaken at Coalbrookdale during the early period, but at the same time he seems to have been experimenting with the use of coke to smelt iron.

Despite the use of coke in other industries, charcoal had remained the favourite fuel for smelting iron as it had fewer impurities. However, the amount of charcoal needed for iron smelting was a serious drawback, and there would clearly be advantages if coke could be used. With an old charcoal blast furnace, Abraham Darby began using coke in 1709, but it is clear from the new research that Darby undertook several years of experimentation with different types of coal, trying to overcome the problems created by impurities in them. It was not until 1715 that he finally discovered that only one sort of coal would be suitable for making iron – the Clod Coal. This coal remained the favourite – and indeed the only – coal used in smelting until well into the nineteenth century (see Chapter 3).

As well as brass founding and ironmaking, there were a variety of other industries attracted to the area by the easy availability of coal. The most unpleasant of these was lead smelting. There were at least four lead smelters here in the mid-eighteenth century, all located on the riverside, using local coal to smelt lead ore imported from Wales via the river Severn. As lead smelting produces poisonous by-products, the smelters would have killed most of the surrounding vegetation and probably affected the local water supply (15). One smelter can be seen in George Robertson's painting of the Iron Bridge, set on the riverbank, and belching smoke.

Martin Eele's tar vats further downstream at Jackfield would have been equally unpleasant, and indeed have left a thick tarry deposit in the surrounding area. In the 1630s he had been extracting tar from local coal, to be used in waterproofing boats. Further along the river to the east at the Salthouses, just beyond the present Jackfield Tile Museum, salt was produced. Brine occurred naturally in one of the geological seams, and the salt was extracted by boiling the brine in vats using coal as fuel.

Neither of these industries was long lived; however, the manufacture of bricks and pottery using local coals and clays persisted until well into the twentieth century. Brick production and pottery making had been established by the beginning of the seventeenth century, but by the early eighteenth century both industries seem to have been using coal as a fuel, and both continued to use local coal well after ironworking had ceased. Another clay industry to make use of local coal was the manufacture of clay tobacco pipes, for which Broseley became famous. Tobacco was introduced in the sixteenth century, but smoking only became widespread in the seventeenth century. The local white clays proved suitable for pipes, and pipemaking became a subsidiary employment among the industrial populations of Broseley Wood and other parts of the Gorge (see Chapters 4 and 5).

These small-scale industries – in which Darby's early ironworks can certainly be included – mark the beginning of a phase of transformation from a coal industry which was largely export-orientated, to one which supplied the demands of a new, local market.

Coal and the Industrial Revolution

The trend towards utilizing coal locally, rather than exporting it, was most marked after the 1750s, when the construction of at least eight blast furnaces in the Gorge created a huge demand for coal. These furnaces were worked by companies which integrated coal-mining into their overall operations, vastly increasing the scale and level of investment in mining. In other words, there was an industrial revolution in the coal industry – mining operations had moved from being the responsibility of individual entrepreneurs or agents, to that of companies with the capital to invest in large-scale operations.

One of the best sources of evidence for the scale and nature of mining during the Industrial Revolution is a map of an estate in Broseley, compiled in 1728 but with additions in 1765.

15 *Lead smelter at the Bower Yard. The fumes would have poisoned much of the surrounding vegetation* (Michael Vanns/Judith Dobie).

16 *A view of the mouth of a coal pit near Broseley, 1788 by Francis Chesham. A horse gin winds coal up the shaft, while a partly loaded waggon waits to take coal down a set of rails. The chimney to the right is for mine ventilation* (IGMT AE 185.770).

Mining on the estate was undertaken by the Willey company which was producing coal for its iron furnaces. The map shows pits and railways and even gives an idea of the extent of underground mining.

It shows that a new mining technique was in use – dotted lines and dates indicate huge areas of working, very much larger than the narrow tunnels and galleries of the seventeenth-century insets. This technique was known as Long Wall mining – coal was taken out from a long working face approached by a network of galleries and the waste (or gob) was packed into the area behind to support the roof. The Best (or Clod), the Flint and sometimes the Middle Coal seams were being worked. The shafts were in pairs, for example, the Jolly and Bonny pits, as well as the Cornbatch Up Pit and the Cornbatch Down Pit; the former

remained in use by a tile-making firm into the twentieth century, and one of the latter pits survives in Cornbatch Dingle today. These pits were all linked to the riverside by a system of railways (see Chapter 8), but it seems also that underground waggonways were used to bring coal from the face to the shafts.

The scale of mining on this estate was typical of the rest of the Gorge where ironworking companies had taken over most of the responsibility for coal-mining. It was part of a general move to integrate all industrial activities – supplying their own coal and other goods rather than relying on others. Coal-mining remained the most important of these activities; several ironworking partnerships were founded on the fortunes made from coal-mining, and at times mining was more economically successful than ironworking.

Eighteenth-century mining remains
Capital was poured into mining operations, leaving a variety of remains of which the most visible are surface remains of the equipment used to pump water out of the mines, or to bring men and coal to the surface. Occasionally it is possible to identify the circular flattened

17 *Pumping engine at the Lloyds coal shaft, 1912. The additional wheel was used to lift the pumprods out of the shaft for repair. To the left is a horse gin winding another shaft (Ron Miles).*

area where a horse walked round and round, operating a winding drum lifting coal, men or buckets of water from a mine (16). Although superseded by steam engines, horse gins remained in use until well into the twentieth century.

There is also evidence for the steam engines which, from the early 1700s, were used to pump water, and later to wind coal up from the pits. The remains of a pumping engine can be seen in the woods at the Lloyds (17), where excavations in 1970 revealed a brick-lined shaft from which a wooden beam protruded, as well as the base of the building which would have contained the engine. The building is very similar to one or two other buildings in the Jackfield area which have now been converted to houses. During renovation of one house near The Tuckies, it was found that the floor joists had been cut away to house a cylinder, and there was a large opening in the rear of the building, opposite an old shaft. The building had been an engine house for the local colliery in the 1780s. A problem for archaeologists is that these engine houses are of little help in identifying the engines themselves; despite improvements in engines in the 1770s, the houses they stood in barely changed.

At Blists Hill there are remains of an engine which can be identified – a Heslop engine (18–20). Adam Heslop was a local mine employee who designed a new type of engine in the 1790s, which was made and used locally for over a hundred years. One of these existed at Blists Hill; known as 'Eve', it was used for pumping water out of a mine shaft there until 1912. It is still possible to see the round 'haystack' boiler bases, the pit where the engine sat and the base of one of the buildings. Nearby were found remains of plateways and parts of the mine headgear and shaft. To the north, a winding engine and mine headgear have been reconstructed by the museum on the base of an original shaft top and building.

Another category of mining evidence found around Blists Hill, and indeed elsewhere in the Gorge, is pieces of mine chain – hand-made wrought-iron chain with rectangular links. Usually three chains were used together, with wooden chocks holding the links together to create a flat chain which would not tangle on the drum as it wound men down a mine or lifted coal out of it. The triple link chain had been invented in 1810, it was much safer than conventional chain and was used until it was replaced by wire rope in the 1870s. Such chain was made at a site at the road junction at the bottom of Blists Hill.

The most spectacular of all the remains in the Gorge associated with coal-mining, and the only one which can be safely entered by the public, is the Tar Tunnel at Coalport (21). Here the visitor can walk about 100m (328ft) along a brick-lined tunnel running into the hillside, and see thick, black pools of bitumen, which have oozed out of the natural rock strata.

In fact the Tar Tunnel originated as an underground canal dug in 1786 to bring coal directly out of the coal shafts at Blists Hill, thus avoiding having to wind coal to the surface and then get it down to the riverside. However, 275m (900ft) into the tunnel, the excavators struck fossil tar – a bituminous substance occurring naturally in the rock strata and used for caulking boats, extracting varnish or for medicinal purposes (of which the survivor today is coal tar soap). Tunnelling ceased, and the tar was collected and boiled in cauldrons to become pitch. Initially a hundred barrels a day were collected, and although the flow had reduced by 1799, commercial exploitation continued into the 1850s.

The tunnel was later extended to the base of the Blists Hill shafts, and after tar extraction stopped was used for mine drainage. Although it may have been used to bring out coal, the Hay Inclined Plane constructed soon after the Tar Tunnel provided an alternative means of getting coal down the steep hillside (see Chapter 8).

Coal-mining in the nineteenth century

The scale of coal-mining in the Gorge decreased dramatically with the exhaustion of the Clod Coal in the early nineteenth century. Ironmasters were turning to new sources of coal in the northern part of the coalfield, around the area which is now Telford. Yet mining continued as an adjunct to other industries such as lime-burning, clay pipemaking and brickmaking and even farming. Such users could afford to be less particular about coal seams than ironmasters and seem to have been using the poorer quality sulphurous coals which the ironmasters had shunned. Mining had become a very makeshift operation – accidents were frequent, ventilation poor, and there are many accounts of old steam engines, horse gins and

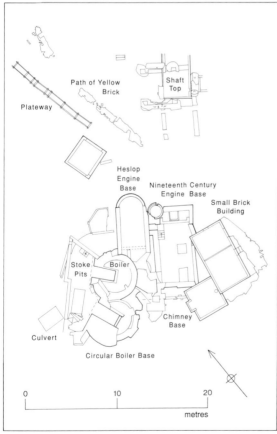

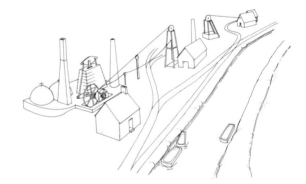

18 (Top) *Coke-making at Blists Hill. In the background the rounded haystack boilers of the Heslop engine can be seen* (IGMT 1982.3040).

19 (Left) *Plan of the excavated Heslop engine base. A later engine base has partly obscured the original layout* (David Higgins/Michael Trueman).

20 (Above) *Reconstruction of the Heslop engine as it might have looked. Once dismantled, an engine leaves a cryptic footprint which may be difficult to interpret, particularly if the engine was altered or replaced several times* (Shelley White).

even hand-operated equipment in use. Mining was in decline; in the 1880s many of the collieries had recently fallen into disuse and by 1902 most were closed apart from large pits such as Granville and Kemberton to the north of the Gorge. During coal shortages – such as the coal strike of 1912 (**22**), and later during the wars – local pits were re-opened, but this was on a small scale.

Coal and the landscape

It is often assumed that coal-mining has ruined the landscape, leaving a legacy of unusable land and old spoil heaps. Coal indeed has caused some damage, although the main culprit is in fact ironstone mining – very little of the waste from coal-mining made its way to the surface. Nevertheless, the impact of coal-mining on the Gorge can be seen in more subtle ways. Coal-mining reshaped the landscape by creating a network of railways, a fleet of barges and what were almost new towns, populated by industrialized miners. In turn coal attracted new industries which meant that coal was used locally rather than exported, creating a basis and indeed some of the capital for the massive expansion in the iron industry which took place in the eighteenth century.

21 *Plateway waggon in the Tar Tunnel (IGMT 1991.923).*

22 *Getting coal during the coal strike, c.1912: a family group sets off from Cape St, Broseley Wood to find coal (IGMT 1984.3219).*

3

Iron and the Industrial Revolution

Today the Ironbridge Gorge is a calm, wooded valley, with little sign of industry, yet during the eighteenth century the area was one of the largest producers of iron in Britain (**23**). Huge blast furnaces belched smoke and flames into the night, and hammers rang on iron against the roar of bellows. Lime kilns gave out an eery light, coke hearths smoked and great white gashes were cut into the surrounding hillsides. Contemporary descriptions evoke images of a hell on earth (**colour plate 4**), the workers emerging blackened and tired, slaves to the constant demands of the furnaces. In contrast to this are our impressions of the ironmasters – stern Quakers, with a clear faith and a strong business ethic.

Archaeology can provide little insight into the individuals who created these ironworks and kept them going, but it is possible to see where they lived and worked and also to begin to answer some of the important questions about the history of ironworking. What was it that first attracted Abraham Darby I to Coalbrookdale? Why did the iron industry suddenly 'take-off' in the years between 1755 and 1780 when at least five new groups of furnaces were set up? Finally, why did the ironworks close and move elsewhere, and the Gorge revert to a rural valley rather than become a Birmingham or a Black Country?

The three surviving groups of iron furnaces mark these different phases in the local iron industry – the earliest, the Darby Furnace at Coalbrookdale represents the change from charcoal to coke as a smelting fuel and was also where the iron for the Iron Bridge was produced seventy years later. Bedlam Furnaces (begun 1756–7) were the first of the great new Industrial Revolution furnaces (**colour plate**

5), experimenting with new forms of power, while the Blists Hill Furnaces, begun in *c*.1832 and closed in 1912, signal the move away from water as a source of power, and eventually the end of smelting in the Gorge. Although smelting has ceased, the Glynwed works still cast parts for boilers and stoves on the lower part of the original Coalbrookdale works.

The archaeology of ironworking is a very diverse subject; it relies on landscapes and buildings just as much as the remains of the furnaces themselves. The blast furnace was only one part of a complex operation which would have included forges, foundries, mills, workshops and subsidiary buildings. Pools, water courses and sluice gates document the way an ironworks was powered, while the housing for ironmasters and workers provides some insight into the social context of the iron industry.

The take-off in iron production in the 1750s was one of the key factors in the Industrial Revolution; reliable supplies of iron were needed for the engines, machinery and buildings of rapidly expanding industries. Thus the events in Coalbrookdale and the rest of the Gorge are of direct relevance to our whole understanding of this momentous period in British history.

Raw materials

In a blast furnace, ironstone, charcoal or coke and limestone are burnt together to produce liquid iron. Bellows blow air into the furnace to keep the temperature up, carbon in the fuel combines with the oxygen in the ore and is blown off as a gas and the other impurities combine with limestone to form a scum which floats to the top of the molten iron. When the

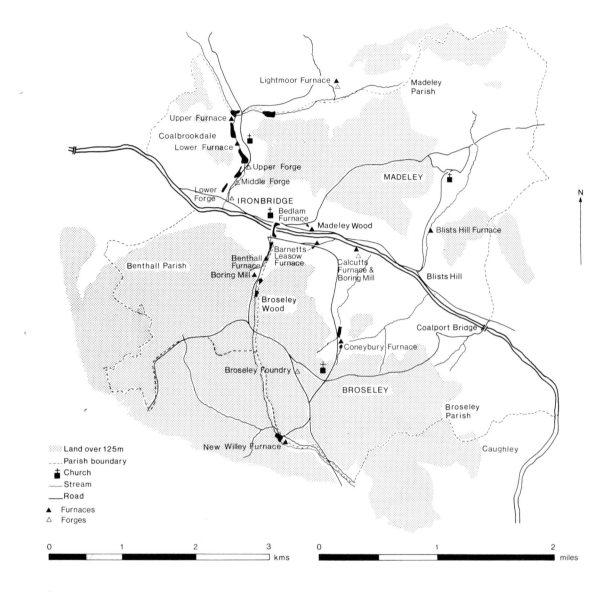

23 *Ironworking sites* (Judith Dobie).

furnace is 'tapped', the slag runs out as a liquid, and the the iron is drawn off into channels in the bed of casting sand which surrounds the furnace.

All the raw materials needed for iron smelting were to be found locally. Suitable coals occur within the Coal Measures, and Lincoln Hill and Benthall Edge are huge outcrops of limestone, initially quarried at the surface and later mined from underground caverns (see Chapter 6).

The other ingredient was ironstone, which occurs in two seams within the Coal Measures – the Crawstone and the Pennystone. These seams are very different; the Crawstone is an iron-rich sandstone, mined in lumps from adits, such as the one surviving in Ironbridge. In contrast, the Pennystone ironstone consists of small flat nodules of ironstone in a matrix of grey clay. The clay was brought to the surface and left to weather, after which pit girls would pick out the ironstone nodules by hand (**colour plate 6**). Crawstone working produced relatively little waste, but Pennystone mines created huge heaps of clay. These heaps can still be seen today in the woods at Ladywood and at the north end of the Free Bridge, where one remains with two small houses perched on top. Mining one ton of ironstone produced nearly 10 tons of spoil, while a ton of coal would produce only half its weight in spoil, so that in fact the bulk of the spoil heaps which once covered this landscape, and indeed much of Telford, were actually the remains of ironstone working.

Pennystone and Crawstone also had different properties, something the ironmasters were aware of from an early date. The quality of iron depends upon the raw materials which are put into the furnace, and it has already been shown that ironmasters would only use one sort of coal for smelting. Abraham Darby's accounts book for the Old Furnace at Coalbrookdale specifies quantities of 'Flatt' and 'Baull' stones in varying proportions, suggesting that he was also experimenting with different ironstone mixtures in the furnace charge.

Ironworking in Coalbrookdale

The earliest ironworking in the Gorge took place at Coalbrookdale where two streams joined and dropped down to the river Severn at the bottom of the valley. At the top of the valley, just below a pool created by the junction of these streams, a Museum of Iron has been created on the site where Abraham Darby first smelted iron using coke and not charcoal.

Underneath a modern triangular building (see 101) at the Coalbrookdale museum site is his blast furnace. It is possible to walk up a new iron staircase and look down into the furnace, where barrow loads of coke, ironstone and limestone would have been dropped into the smoking hole. Like most Shropshire furnaces, this was built into a bank so that raw materials could be fed directly into the top of the furnace (24). The centre of the furnace is lined with white brick, which was better able to withstand the high temperatures than ordinary red brick. Down below was the tuyere arch, where great bellows would have fed air into a small opening (or tuyere) in the front of the furnace. A faint curved scratch in the stone can just be seen on one side of this arch, cut by the water-wheel which powered the bellows, and further around the base of the furnace is the second opening from which molten slag and pure iron would have been drawn out, running into

channels cut in black casting sand on the ground.

Four iron beams support the brickwork above the first of these arches. Two bear the name and date, 'ABRAHAM.DARBY.1777', and the other a curious B E, a crown, the date 1658 and the initials EB. When Abraham Darby first came here in 1708, he took over a busy ironworking site with an old charcoal blast furnace which had been operated by the landowner Basil Brooke of Madeley and his wife Elizabeth, probably the names referred to by the initials (25). Darby was able to convert the furnace to the use of coke rather than charcoal and to produce iron successfully.

This same furnace remained in blast for many years. However, when the Iron Bridge was being planned in the 1770s, it was realized that a bigger furnace was needed to produce the iron for the bridge. The old furnace was rebuilt to give it a greater capacity, the arches enlarged, and two new beams inserted by Abraham Darby III, then in control of the works.

In the days of Abraham Darby I, the furnace site would have looked very different to its appearance today. Most of the site was devoted to processes relating to casting – the furnace would have been surrounded by buildings to protect the wheel, the bellows and the molten iron from the weather. Wooden patterns for the casting-moulds were made in pattern shops, there would have been mills for grinding the ingredients for the black casting sand, and stacked at the top of the furnace would have been baskets of coke, raw materials and old iron ready to be put into the furnace.

None of these buildings stands today, and in fact most of the remains on the site are much later. To the east of the Old Furnace stands the Snapper furnace, built in 1805 to provide extra capacity but never used; most of its bricks were robbed out during the Second World War. On the other side stand two walls; these enclosed a water-wheel that last worked this century, powering the grinding wheel situated behind it.

The two buildings still standing are the Great Warehouse of 1838, now used as the Museum of Iron, and the Long Warehouse built by 1902, which houses the Ironbridge Institute and the museum library. Although iron smelting ceased at this site in 1816, the Coalbrookdale site remained in use for producing ornamental art castings. Typical of this output was the decorative clock of 1843, placed on top of the Great

24 *Reconstruction of the Darby Furnace, Coalbrookdale. The water wheel operated bellows which pushed air into the furnace. Coke, ironstone and limestone were placed into the top of the furnace and molten iron and slag were drawn off from the bottom. Shropshire furnaces were normally built into a bank – in this case the dam of the pool* (Judith Dobie).

Warehouse at the southern end of the site. The Great Warehouse must have towered over the motley collection of single-storey sheds, as a proud symbol of the company's new prosperity and success in the nineteenth century. Beside it the Long Warehouse was used to store the rather more mundane productions of the early twentieth century – such as stoves for council houses or rainwater goods such as gutters and down-pipes.

Ironworking gradually stopped at this site as the company concentrated its operations lower down the valley, and in Ketley (now part of Telford) to the north. In 1959, for the 250th anniversary of the Coalbrookdale Company, the debris around the furnace was cleared and the site opened to the public. A small museum was opened near the furnace, and in 1970 the site became part of the Ironbridge Gorge Museum complex.

Housing

Clustered around the Coalbrookdale ironworks are the houses of those who worked there, both as employees and ironmasters. These houses reveal a little of the aspirations and attitudes of those who built them, and something of how Coalbrookdale functioned as a community.

On the hillside above the works stand two early eighteenth-century houses – Rosehill and Dale House (**colour plate 2**). Dale House was begun in 1715 by Abraham Darby I for his family, and after his death two years later was occupied by many different people, including the ironmaster Richard Reynolds, Abraham Darby II and III and also many of the works

25 *Interior of the Abraham Darby Furnace moulding shop at the Upper Works, Coalbrookdale c.1880–90 with the Old Furnace in the background. The furnace arch is used for shelving. The initials of Basil and Elizabeth Brooke can be seen* (IGMT 1984.6749).

managers. Rosehill was begun in the 1730s for Richard Ford, manager of the works after Darby's death.

The Darbys and the Reynolds were Quakers, adhering strictly to the ideals of self-discipline, frugality and simple faith, attitudes which extended into the conduct of their business. As members of the Society of Friends, Quakers formed a close-knit group, distinct in their way of dress and habits, and tending to socialize as a group. Many of the visitors who came to Coalbrookdale were Quaker associates, and the large houses at Coalbrookdale became a focus for this society.

The houses were built close to the works, but looked out over a more pleasant view of trees, pleasure gardens and a pool with a small decorative iron bridge (**colour plate 2**). For most of their history the houses were occupied for relatively short periods by family members or by works managers; often, as in the case of Abraham Darby III, while they built or altered finer houses elsewhere in more rural settings (**27**).

The company also built housing at Coalbrookdale for their employees. In 1700 the whole village had consisted of one furnace, five

26 *Coalbrookdale Company employees at the Upper Works* c.*1901* (IGMT 1981.3021).

dwellings and a forge or two, but within forty years there was housing for at least 450 people and employment for 500. Most of these houses would have been small brick one-and-a-half-storey cottages, built for individual workers by local builders, but some were company-built. Carpenters Row (**28**) is an example of company housing; built c.1783, it is a terrace of eight cottages, each with a downstairs parlour with a range, a tiny pantry and a bedroom above.

There was originally a brewhouse at either end of the row – a communal area where some of the messier household tasks such as brewing beer, laundry or butchering animals might take place. Such terraces would have provided accommodation for skilled or semi-skilled workers, as well as being a sound investment for the company itself.

When it was built, Carpenters Row would have provided a relatively good class of accommodation, but in the nineteenth century back kitchens and bedrooms were added to make the units larger. There was a demand for better and larger accommodation, and around Coalbrookdale it is possible to see a steady growth in the nineteenth century in the number of

The Hay, Madeley

27 *The Hay, Madeley, photographed c.1900–20. The seventeenth-century house was bought by Abraham Darby III in 1781, who altered it substantially. It looks across the river to The Tuckies, a house occupied by Earl Dundonald who experimented with tar production, and later by the innovator William Reynolds (IGMT 1985.166).*

small houses, built perhaps for artisans whose skills were well rewarded and who thus had the means to purchase them.

The community that developed at Coalbrookdale could never be called a town for it lacked the variety of trades found in nearby Ironbridge or Madeley. Instead it remained largely an ironworking community, focused around the employment and social network provided by the works.

Ironworking in the Coalbrookdale Valley

The Upper Works was only one of five different ironworking sites which stretched down the valley. Relatively little research has been done on the archaeology of these sites, partly because most of them lie deeply buried under several metres of ash and ironworking debris which built up from the furnaces. What does survive above ground is an interesting group of buildings, some not obviously industrial, which all represent different facets of the iron industry.

To the south was the Lower Works, where Abraham Darby I added a second iron furnace in 1715. Iron is still cast here in a series of modern sheds, and although the earlier furnace has gone the site includes some important Victorian buildings. At the top of the site is the Engineering Shop and a complex which housed the company offices and drawing areas, and at the bottom of the site is a remarkable building with a nine-ridged hipped roof. The complex provides evidence for the development of the company and how its need for space and buildings changed during the nineteenth century, perhaps the least well understood period of its operation.

28 *Carpenters Row* (centre) *built c.1783 for Coalbrookdale Company employees. A brewhouse or area for washing and other domestic tasks formerly stood at either end of the building. The cottage gardens may be seen in the front* (IGMT 1992.6195).

The oldest ironworking building survives at the next site down the valley – the Upper Forge (**29**). Now mostly grassed over and used for picnics, the site was once covered with small furnaces, engines and buildings, as well as the house where Abraham Darby lived when he first came to the Gorge. It was at this site that pig iron was converted into wrought iron in a forge by heating and hammering. Because it was malleable and could be shaped, wrought iron was far more useful than cast iron. The one remaining building looks at first sight like a nineteenth-century stable block and mill, but was originally built as a forge in the 1760s or 1770s. The area is of potential archaeological importance for other reasons, as it was here that the Cranage brothers were experimenting with a new process to use coke not charcoal to make wrought iron. It was also the site of a seventeenth-century steel-house, where the

landowner Basil Brooke, who operated the old charcoal furnace higher up the valley, may have been using a process to make steel which he had patented in 1620.

Further down the valley are two rather enigmatic buildings on the site of a fourth ironworks known as the Middle Forge. A timber-framed building, now known as Rose Cottages, may have been industrial in origin (**30**). The cottages have a porch dated to 1634 added, and it is possible that this building might have had links with an earlier smithy in the valley, noted in 1544. The building to the rear of the cottages is also problematic; it is a small, high shed built of handmade brick, and set upon earlier foundations. In 1734 there was a boring mill here, used to grind engine cylinders, and by 1780 it had been rebuilt to a design by John Wilkinson, an ironmaster on the south bank of the river. Whether this is the 1780 boring mill, or simply a later nineteenth-century shed remains open to debate.

Finally, at the bottom of the Dale is the site of the Lower Forge, used in 1694 for hammering frying pans from plates of iron. Nail-making had taken over from frying pan manufacture by 1838, and the site later became a tramway depot and warehouse. Most of the early forge

(a)

(b)

29 *The Upper Forge, Coalbrookdale. This is the only known eighteenth-century ironworking building in the Gorge. Archaeological analysis of the fabric combined with documentary evidence has shown that it was originally built as a forge in the 1760s or 1770s (a). A tower (rear) was added to house a Boulton & Watt steam engine installed in 1787 to work the bellows of the forge (b). By 1847 the front of the building had been remodelled and it was in use as a stables and mill (c). A water-wheel (not visible) had been added to the rear – an example of using the most appropriate, rather than the most up to date technology. (Judith Dobie).*

(c)

30 *Rose Cottages* (right) *and to the rear, the workshop built on the foundations of an earlier boring mill* (Michael Worthington).

has gone apart from an extraordinary timber roof structure now found under an unremarkable modern tiled roof (**31**).

At the back of a present-day petrol station is a stone wall, the remains of part of the dam for the pool which supplied the Lower Forge. In order to function, these sites required power – to work forge hammers, push bellows, turn slitting mills or bore cannon. Each of these sites was located below a pool, holding water from the local stream. A study of this pool system reveals some interesting anomalies in the decision-making process in the eighteenth-century iron industry.

Water-power in Coalbrookdale

In 1754, a visitor Charles Wood remarked that 'There is the most work done at these places with the least water of any place in England'; while in 1815 Thomas Butler saw 'Two furnaces, Darby & Co both in blast. These furnaces are blown by a water wheel, all the machinery old and clumsy and all the works seem to be conducted on the old plans of forty years ago'.

These two quotations sum up the conundrum of Coalbrookdale – on the one hand the company was in the forefront of ironworking, in touch with the latest steam-engine technology, and on the other, it continued to use an outdated water-power system, not only in 1815, but well into the twentieth century.

In 1708 Abraham Darby had found not only an old furnace, but a system of four pools with an additional reservoir at the top, to which he added another reservoir to power the New Furnace in 1715. In the 1730s the company had

31 *Roof truss with cast-iron support, Coalbrookdale; an unexpected piece of industrial archaeology. The iron beam* (right) *comprises a three-sided trough containing a length of timber; together the materials give a combination of strength in tension and compression* (Michael Worthington).

trouble keeping the furnaces in blast during summer water shortages, so they installed a horse-powered pump to lift water back through the pools after it was used. The system was successful, and was replaced in 1742 by a steam engine, located by the former Methodist Chapel. In 1781 the company made an even bigger investment in the existing system, building what was then the largest engine ever constructed. Called 'Resolution', it pumped water along a tunnel half a mile long from the

Boring Mill pool, up shafts of 37m (120ft) into a culvert leading to the Upper Furnace Pool. New technology kept the old system of wheels and pools in operation. Although the engine went out of use when smelting ceased, water-wheels remained a source of power well into the twentieth century – most recently to drive a generator at the petrol station in the 1930s. Instead of installing the steam technology then available to blow furnaces directly, the company had adapted and kept going an old system that nevertheless represented a large investment in dams and equipment.

Abraham Darby I had clearly been attracted to the area, not just by the availability of raw materials, but by the advantages of water-power, as well as an already existing ironworks, with blast furnace, pools and forges. By the nineteenth century, these initial attractions had become major disadvantages. Had the Coalbrookdale Company built their works on a greenfield site instead of one which was medieval in origin, the pattern of working and the decisions taken might have been very different.

Bedlam Furnaces

Between 1756 and 1760 an extraordinary change took place – nine new blast furnaces were built within the Gorge, and the area became one of the largest producers of iron in the country. The Coalbrookdale works had operated on a modest scale, using one old blast furnace and a new furnace. Suddenly, production expanded in an unprecedented fashion. What had happened to cause this?

One factor must have been a new technological development in iron-making. Most iron production had remained dependent upon charcoal as a fuel; industry needed wrought iron not pig iron, and iron made with coke could not be converted into wrought iron so charcoal-fired furnaces were still needed. As a result of experiments at Coalbrookdale with different iron ores, however, the art of making a coke-iron which *could* be converted to wrought iron was perfected. The new furnaces were able for the first time to supply large quantities of iron to the forges using coke as a fuel.

The second factor was the use of new forms of power. This is best illustrated at Bedlam Furnaces, which lie between Ironbridge and Coalport and were built by the Madeley Wood Company in 1756-7 (**colour plates 3, 4** and **5**). Unlike the furnaces at Coalbrookdale, Bedlam was not located on a stream, but adjacent to the river Severn. Water was pumped out of the river with a steam engine, and fed back over water-wheels which powered the bellows. In other words, the water-wheel was kept going with a steam engine. The system neatly overcame the problems which had been encountered at Coalbrookdale with seasonal water shortages as there was always water in the river (although river levels fluctuated too much to be used directly). Steam and water power were neatly combined in one system, with the added advantage that the furnace could continue working even if the steam engine was broken. The same principle was used at other furnaces, where engines recycled water from tiny streams which would never have had the volume of water or the height to keep a traditional furnace going. With more reliable blast, these new furnaces could be bigger, and produce more iron than their predecessors.

Bedlam is the only one of a whole group of furnaces built in the 1750s to have survived – those at Horsehay, Lightmoor, New Willey and Ketley to the north have all now been demolished. In losing these furnaces, we have lost information about precisely what happened to the design of furnaces as the ironmasters adapted the new technology. Such experiments are rarely documented, and can only be understood from the archaeology of the furnace.

Another experimental, and somewhat enigmatic, site has been excavated at Newdale, to the north of the Gorge, prior to opencast coal-mining (**32**). Documentary evidence suggested that this was the site of the 'New Dale', created by the Coalbrookdale Company in the 1750s when they were having problems with their leases. Detailed recording showed that the two surviving buildings were open sheds, supported on iron columns, and purpose built for iron-working. A casting pit and the remains of small furnaces suggested that iron was being re-melted here for casting.

Archaeology has shown that Newdale had been planned as the beginning of a much larger settlement. As well as the two standing buildings, archaeologists found remains of a group of others, including another forge building, and a row of back-to-back cottages laid out in a group of fields on a similar alignment (**33**). Such cottages are more commonly associated with industrial towns, where space was scarce and people were packed into a small area, and imply that the company had grand designs for the complex. For some reason the ironworking project was abandoned soon after it had begun, and the remaining buildings became a small coal-mining settlement during the nineteenth century.

Bedlam, Newdale, the Upper Forge and the other sites of the 1750s and 1760s are sites of great significance. These were two of the most important decades in the history of ironworking, when new technologies were tried out. Something happened in ironworking that gave investors enough faith to build expensive new works in a very short period. Experiments and failures were rarely documented, and only archaeology will enable us to reconstruct what might have been.

The missing south bank furnaces

Because the best preserved sites are on the north bank of the river, it is easy to forget that

32 *Two ironworking buildings at Newdale dated to 1759 and now demolished. Two air furnaces lay between the buildings and were used for casting* (Mark Horton/Michael Worthington).

33 *Excavated eighteenth-century back-to-back cottages, Newdale* (Mark Horton/Michael Worthington).

there were as many works on the south bank, none of which remain standing. It is a salutary lesson for archaeologists that a huge blast furnace, with its outbuildings and vast output of waste, can disappear without trace within 150 years. The furnaces at Calcutts (**34**), built in 1767 to take advantage of new canals further down the Severn linking this area with the Black Country, now lie under a modern house, and those at Coneybury are little more than a few faint humps in a grassy field. The Broseley furnace is not visible, and the Barnett's Leasow furnace of 1797 has vanished, leaving only a few tell-tale lumps of slag in a garden wall.

34 An Iron Work for Casting Cannon, *by Wilson Lowry (1762–1824) after George Robertson (1724–88), showing the Calcutts Furnaces on the south bank of the river. A house has now been built on the site* (IGMT AE 185.760).

In the Benthall valley above the Iron Bridge there was once an ironworks employing 700 people. Nothing survives of the furnaces, but there is a landscape which is just as interesting as Coalbrookdale, with the same pattern of alternating pools and water-power sites. Here the valley is steeper, and the stream was smaller, yet there was a boring mill, ironworks and foundry as well as several corn mills, one with a huge water-wheel.

Blists Hill and the end of iron smelting

The last furnaces in the Gorge were at Blists Hill (**35** and **colour plate 7**). After Bedlam Furnaces closed in about the 1830s, the Madeley Wood Company erected new furnaces at Blists Hill. Coal and ironstone were having to be brought from further and further away, and the new furnaces were close to productive mines. They were also close to the canal, which had

49

35 *Blists Hill Furnaces redrawn from a late nineteenth-century photograph. In 1874 the furnaces were raised and their tops closed in to improve productivity. Today the engine houses to the left and right survive as well as the furnace bases and the buildings behind them. The casting houses in front have been demolished* (Shelley White).

taken over from the river Severn as the main means of transporting iron.

By this date steam engines were used directly to blow air into the furnace, without any need for water-wheels. Two great engine houses can be seen on either side of the furnaces, one with the opening for the air pipe which would have led to the furnace. Only the bases of the three furnaces survive – one built in 1832, the others in 1840 and 1844. Behind them are the arches of the smiths shops – buildings housing various maintenance activities. In front of the buildings there would have been casting houses, but these have now disappeared.

Blists Hill Furnaces closed in 1912 – they were still operating on the cold blast principle, a process which had long been superseded by the introduction of hot blast, whereby the air was heated before being forced into the furnace. More importantly, steel had now replaced

wrought iron as the major construction material. Many claimed that the iron was of a superior quality, and the company improved production levels by closing in the tops of the furnaces in 1874. Nevertheless, most of the raw materials now came from elsewhere and the market for the product was diminishing. This was the last time that iron was smelted in the Gorge.

Casting and other processes continued – most of the stoves for the early twentieth-century boom in London houses came from Coalbrookdale, and since then Aga stoves and other items have been made. But there were no longer any real advantages to the Gorge – the river was unnavigable, transport had become difficult, raw materials and markets lay elsewhere. The natural advantages which had drawn Abraham Darby to the Gorge now served to create an industrial backwater.

The Industrial Revolution of the eighteenth century was the one period when events in Britain were to transform much of the rest of the world. Britain was not an outpost, as during the period of Roman rule, it was the centre, the place where a revolution in industry took place. One factor in the Industrial Revolution was undoubtedly the new ability to produce large supplies of usable iron. Many of the developments which led to this took place in the Gorge.

The Iron Bridge was built at the height of this ironworking boom, and was promoted by local industrialists who were anxious to show the rest of the world what had been achieved. But it is not a bridge in isolation – its context is the landscape of the Gorge with all its advantages and disadvantages, the thriving coal industry which preceded iron, the transport links and the investment which had already gone into the landscape, and of course the people – the communities who had created and sustained the transformation of an isolated wooded valley.

One of the industries which had long supported such communities was the manufacture of pottery and clay pipes. It is often forgotten that industries such as coal-mining, ironworking and particularly barge-hauling – pulling the boats which carried goods to markets in the south – were seasonal and depended on such factors as the weather or levels of rainfall. Workers would be idle for part of the year, so the manufacture of pottery or tobacco pipes became a form of by-employment. Yet the ceramic industry – like coal production and the iron industry – underwent its own form of industrial revolution, epitomized by the world-famous Coalport China Works.

4

From chamber pots to gilded urns

The best known pottery in the Ironbridge Gorge is the Coalport China Works; here, fine porcelains fit to grace the tables of aristocrats were produced throughout the nineteenth century. The china painters of Coalport gained an international reputation for their skill and artistry, producing elaborate pieces of great elegance for customers such as the Tsar of Russia, the British Royal family and the wealthy London Livery companies. At the Caughley works to the south, their predecessors were credited with the introduction of the blue willow pattern and other designs which are used to this day on fine blue-and-white china. Taking advantage of the late eighteenth-century vogue for drinking tea, they were able to copy the Chinese designs that had become popular earlier in the century but which could not be supplied in sufficient quantities, and thus they supplied a cheaper local product to a ready market.

Less well known are the more mundane potteries making plain, serviceable earthenwares for use in the home or the dairy. Their wares are commonly found on archaeological sites, but unlike Coalport the potteries – and the personalities – are rarely documented. Yet the local pottery industry had a significant role to play in the founding of the better known porcelain works. Well before the Caughley factory was established in 1772 there was a pool of skilled labour, a well-developed knowledge of the local coals and clays and the infrastructure to mine and transport them (36).

Clays

Once again, raw materials are an important part of understanding how the industry operated, and clay, like coal is not a straightforward material – the clays for bricks, roof tiles and pottery were all different. Coalport and Caughley did not make use of local clays, relying instead on fine white China clays from Devon and Cornwall, but local clays were used to manufacture earthenware. There were the white clays, used for clay pipes and perhaps salt-glaze pottery, buff- and red-burning clays used for earthenwares, and refractory clays able to stand great heat used for making saggars and bricks to line furnaces.

Clay was bulkier and of lower value than most of the other minerals in the Gorge, and only begins to be mentioned specifically in mining leases in the nineteenth century. Nevertheless, local clays had been mined since the seventeenth century and had perhaps been used even earlier for the medieval floor tiles found at Buildwas Abbey and Wenlock Priory. Because clay was of such low value, it was rarely worth investing in expensive mines and underground clay mines were rare. The exception to this was when an old coal mine had been worked out, and the shafts and equipment were kept in operation for clay mining. This happened at Blists Hill where the coal shafts of the 1780s were still in use for hauling clay up in the middle of this century.

The only surviving underground clay mine lies part way up Bridge Bank above the Iron Bridge, near the site of the old Maws tileworks, where galleries lined with yellow tiles lead straight into the hillside, and the working faces are just as the last miner left them.

Clay pipemaking

In the seventeenth century white clay tobacco pipes made in Broseley on the south bank of the river were smoked all over Britain. White clay pipes were first made in London during

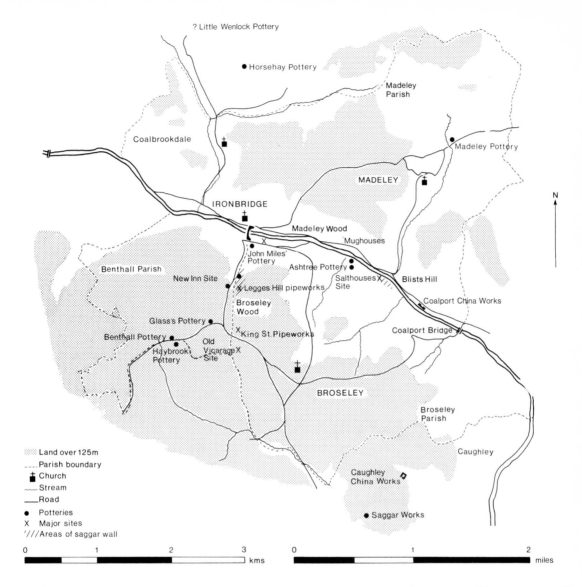

36 *Pottery and clay pipemaking sites* (Judith Dobie).

the later sixteenth century. Smoking spread rapidly to the provinces, and by the 1630s pipemakers had settled around Much Wenlock and Broseley. From the 1650s distinctive local forms emerged. As trade expanded the area became one of the most significant pipemaking centres in the country, sending pipes by road and river to large parts of Staffordshire, Warwickshire, Worcestershire and Wales as well as

America and the Caribbean. Pipes are usually stamped with a maker's mark, and so it is possible to trace where a pipe came from, and often the name of its maker. The Broseley type series (**37**) is one of the major regional styles recognized in England and the forms produced here influenced and were copied by other makers over a wide area.

Pipemaking was carried out on a small scale by individuals or families in their homes until the early nineteenth century when factory-type production was introduced at three sites in the Broseley area – the New Inn site on Bridge Bank, the Legges Hill site and the King Street

53

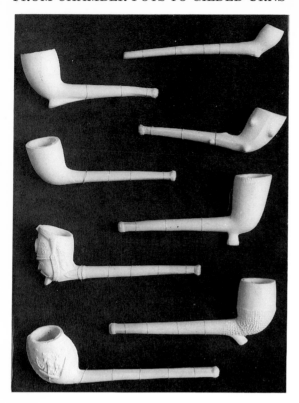

37 *A selection of Broseley clay pipes* (IGMT A 1660).

Pipeworks. With the opening of the railway, pipes were exported all over Britain and abroad. By the later nineteenth century up to a hundred workers were engaged in pipemaking, producing perhaps ten million pipes per year. The last clay pipe factory using traditional methods closed only in 1960. Broseley is therefore one of the most important pipemaking centres in this country. It was a production centre of national importance for over 300 years and the identification and interpretation of its products are of wide interest.

The vanishing local pottery industry
The Ironbridge Gorge does not immediately spring to mind as one of the great centres of post-medieval pottery manufacture of the order of, for example, Stoke-on-Trent. And yet in the early part of the eighteenth century many of the same wares were made, with the same combination of coals and clays, and potters were moving between one area and another. Although all the basic ingredients were here,

the local pottery industry never expanded to rival Stoke-on-Trent, remaining at a small scale throughout the eighteenth and nineteenth centuries.

After ten years of fieldwork it is possible to identify the broad range of post-medieval pottery types which occur in domestic houses and rubbish tips. The problem for the archaeologist is to identify which were actually made here, and which were brought in from elsewhere.

Medieval pottery
The evidence for medieval pottery is, essentially, negative. The lack of medieval pottery confirms the general impression that the Gorge was sparsely populated prior to the seventeenth century. Occasional sherds of coarse earthenware, with a gritty fabric and traces of green glaze, have been found, but there is no evidence for their manufacture.

Salt-glazed stoneware
In the 1720s, Staffordshire potters began making a fine white stoneware, with incised decoration dusted with blue cobalt. In 1981, archaeologists found evidence for the manufacture of similar pottery in the Gorge. Pottery wasters, saggars, pieces of kiln furniture and the burnt flint which would have been used in the body of the ware, were found on the riverside at Jackfield (**38**). The pottery fragments included tankards, plates, bowls and lids which if found in Staffordshire would be dated to the 1730s or 1740s. In the garden walls of houses nearby and also in the neighbourhood of Broseley Wood to the west, are found whole saggars, often with fragments of pottery still clinging to the base.

Poor Law records show that potters had come from Stoke-on-Trent to the Broseley area in 1723-5 to work at two potteries, run by William Bird and Joseph Gardner. Trade had obviously slumped, as in the 1730s at least 13 were claiming poor relief. It is possible that these potters had brought skills learnt in Staffordshire to the Gorge, where they found the white clays and coals needed to fire pottery.

Coarse earthenware
Almost every garden in the area of the Gorge produces pieces of broken slip-decorated earthenware. There are shallow press-moulded dishes with a buff fabric, with brown and yellow decoration coated in a lead glaze, as well as wheel-thrown chamber pots and mugs decor-

39 Group of late eighteenth-century domestic earthenwares made in the area. Clockwise from rear: Pancheon with red fabric, brown slip and clear glaze on interior. Vessel with red fabric, clear glazed interior. Tankard with manganese streaked glaze and turned decoration. Mug with brown and yellow slipped decoration. Press-moulded dish, buff fabric with brown and yellow slipped decoration. Wheel-thrown chamber pot with brown and yellow slipped decoration (Judith Dobie).

5cms

38 Scratch-blue salt-glazed pottery found with kiln furniture and wasters at Jackfield (IGMTAU).

ated in yellow and brown, and chunks of coarse, red-fabric earthenware, with a brown or clear slip in a variety of large forms such as pancheons (**39**). This pottery was relatively cheap, everyday ware, used for preserving, to separate cream in the dairy, in the kitchen or in the brewhouse. Archaeology theoretically enables us to link these wares with the potteries known from documents, but does not yet help to date the ware.

As ever, the documentary evidence cannot quite be reconciled with the field evidence. Direct evidence for manufacture in the form of wasters, comes from Salthouses and from other surface collections, none of which can be related to a specific pottery, whereas at the documented sites, field evidence for manufacturing is scarce.

There were at least three Jackfield potteries in the eighteenth century, shown on the Broseley Hall estate map (**40**). Two, known as the Mughouses, are both made up of a terrace of houses with a pottery kiln at one end, and one, belonging to Morris Thursfield, resembles a more conventional pottery laid out as a courtyard, with a house, a row of buildings and a kiln in one corner. These may be the same three potteries mentioned again in 1773 as belonging to Richard Simpson, Thursfield and Bell, and

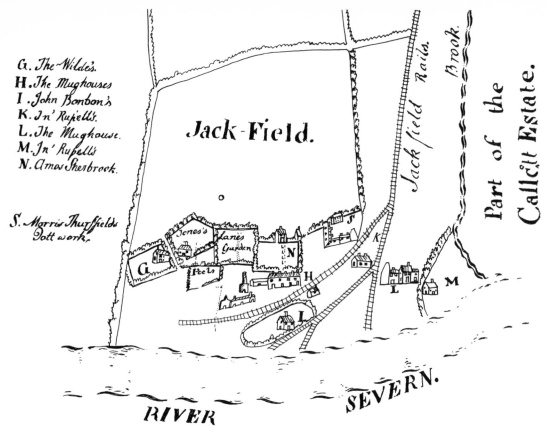

G. *The Wildes.*
H. *The Mughouses*
I. *John Bonbon's*
K. *In' Rupell's.*
L. *The Mughouse.*
M. *In' Rupell's*
N. *Amos Shenbrook.*

S. *Morris Thursfields Pott works.*

Jack-Field.

Part of the Callcil Estate.

Jackfield Rails.

Brook.

RIVER

SEVERN.

40 *Extract from Broseley Hall estate map, 1728/65 showing a pottery and mughouses on the Jackfield riverside. The present Jackfield Tileworks Museum is on the site of 'S' (SBL/Nicola Smith).*

Morris Thursfield. One of these rows of cottages still survives, and there is also a definite concentration of slipware sherds in this area.

Slipwares have also been found at the sites of the other documented potteries, including Caughley, where Ambrose Gallimore had tenure of an earthenware pottery in c.1750–72 and at Little Wenlock where Andrew Bradley had a pottery in 1767. Large quantities of slipwares (but unfortunately no wasters) were also found during the renovation of a cottage at Ladywood, near where John Miles owned a pottery in 1761, described as having a 'round pottery ware work' for wheel-thrown pieces, and a 'flat ware work' for the press-moulded pieces.

Two more potteries in Benthall made slipwares – the Haybrook Pottery and the Benthall Pottery. The Haybrook Pottery was established by 1743 and possibly earlier, and by 1805 consisted of, 'three kilns, hovels [the structure housing the kiln], smoke houses [perhaps drying sheds] and warehouse' and contained a stock of earthenware. Most of the buildings were demolished in the 1960s, and the site used for opencast mining, but some of the pottery waste-heaps survive. Across the road, parts of the Benthall Pottery still stand within an agricultural machinery store. Founded in 1772, the pottery closed only in 1939 when production moved over to salt-glazed sanitary pipes. In 1815 it was

in a compleat state for carrying on a manufactory of common earthenware, and well situated for Land Sale and the trade to Bristol and for Foreign Exportation,

suggesting that pottery was transported by road as well as river, and that there was a good overseas market. The owner of the pottery, Morris Thursfield, had actually died in America while taking a cargo of earthenware there in 1783.

41 *The Caughley Works from a picture published in* The Salopian Monthly Illustrated Journal, *April 1875. The area of the main buildings has been opencast, but the site of the pond and two smaller buildings remains* (IGMT 1986.11057).

Dating slipwares such as these is almost impossible, as they were made over such a long period. Local slipwares lack the raised decoration of seventeenth-century types, suggesting that they are mainly eighteenth century. There is some evidence to suggest that slipwares were still manufactured in the 1880s – John Randall described the pottery as making red and yellow wares – and that even in 1855 the pottery made the 'traditional form of slipware or Welsh dishes for which the Benthall Potteries even today get occasional enquiries'.

Slipwares were also made in great quantities in Stoke-on-Trent, although there are slight typological differences – local wares tend to have a buff body with a dark slip, as opposed to the red body with yellow slip of Stoke. It seems likely that with better transport and larger centres of population nearby, the Stoke potters were able to reach a wider market than the Shropshire potters, whose output seems to have declined after the eighteenth century.

Other earthenwares
It is puzzling that archaeologists have yet to find firm evidence in the form of wasters for the local manufacture of what is known as Jackfield ware – a glossy black ware with a fine red fabric and gilt decoration which is thought to have been produced here. The ware was definitely made in Staffordshire in the period 1730–60, and the local potter Morris Thursfield has been credited with its development at his pottery. It has been claimed that black decanters were indeed made at a local pottery in the early eighteenth century, but only one potential waster has been found.

A single unglazed red teapot lid with white sprigged decoration has been found, resembling a Staffordshire pottery type. There is also some suggestion for the manufacture of tankards, with a streaked iron-rich glaze, found at the Old Vicarage in Benthall and black earthenware wasters have been found at the Legges Hill site in Broseley Wood.

The Caughley Works

Late eighteenth-century pottery manufacture was dominated by the quest to copy the fashionable blue-and-white porcelains imported from China. The Ironbridge Gorge was one area in which such experiments took place.

Soft paste porcelain was first manufactured at Caughley, where in 1772 Thomas Turner of Worcester took over an old earthenware manufactory. He built a new pottery with an elaborate three-storey building, kilns and workshops, laid out around a courtyard (41). There was a saggar works to the south, other small buildings and also pools, and a mill for grinding raw materials at Willey. Some of the porcelain manufactured there was sent elsewhere for decoration at other works, and some was hand painted or transfer-printed with pretty blue Chinese-style designs (42). In 1799 the business was sold to John Rose of Coalport, who carried on the works until they were demolished in 1814.

Most of the site was cleared by opencast mining in the 1960s, and only a few elements remain in a field to the north – coal-mines, the imprint of a horse gin and perhaps the two small buildings and pool shown on an early engraving. At the saggar works to the south archaeologists have found the foundations of buildings, heaps of saggars and an area of surface mining dug into the Ganey and Clod coals (see Chapter 2).

The Caughley site is in an isolated location, surrounded by fields on a hill above the river. It seems an odd place to build a new factory, until one realizes that in 1772 this was a busy area; the network of tramways which linked the coal-mines to the river were immediately put into service supplying the pottery and bringing imported clay up from the riverside. The saggar works remained in operation (43), and labour, perhaps with skills already gained in the earthenware potteries, would have come from the nearby village of Broseley.

Another key to the siting of the Caughley factory may have been the landowner, Ralph Browne, who had a considerable interest both in pottery and also in improving his estate. Soon after the works was constructed, a local farm was remodelled as a home farm for Caughley Hall nearby. Caughley Hall was improved, and Thomas Turner built Caughley Place for himself. This was an elaborate house in the French style, and the same architectural theme

42 *Porcelain cream jug, made at Caughley c.1790* (IGMT).

may have been picked up in the ornate square gatehouse, with a pyramidal roof and brick quoins, which survives on the boundary of the estate (44). The prestige of the Caughley factory and its products were clearly seen as a suitable way of enhancing a landed estate.

Porcelain in Jackfield

In 1983 porcelain wasters, including fluted bowls, were found in a sewage trench at Jackfield. Although the sherds could form an unusual dump from the works downstream at Coalport on the other side of the river, it is also possible that they relate to a brief period in c.1780 when John Rose, an apprentice at Caughley, joined Edward Blakeway in Morris Thursfield's Jackfield pottery, and may well have manufactured porcelain there.

The Coalport China Works

As at Caughley, the concept of a prestigious industry breaking away from local traditions

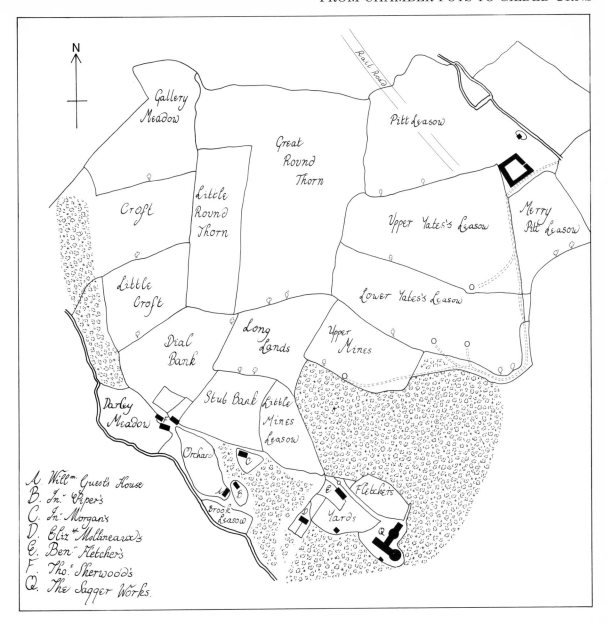

N

Gallery
Meadow

Pitt Leasow

Rail Road

Great
Round
Thorn

Croft

Little
Round
Thorn

Upper Yates's Leasow

Merry
Pitt Leasow

Little
Croft

Lower Yates's Leasow

Dial
Bank

Long
Lands

Upper
Mines

Darley
Meadow

Stub Bank

Little
Mines
Leasow

Orchard

C

A

B

Brook
Leasow

E

Fletchers

D

Yards

Q

A. Willm. Guest's House
B. In^{o.} Piper's
C. In^{o.} Morgan's
D. Elizth Mollineaux's
E. Ben^{n.} Fletcher's
F. Thos Sherwood's
Q. The Sagger Works.

of coarse earthenware manufacture and reaching a national market, can be seen in the china works on the riverside at Coalport (**45** and **colour plate 8**). The Coalport China Works now form the Coalport Museum of China, a group of buildings and kilns housing displays relating to the processes and products of the factory.

The key to the location of the china works was the canal/river interchange, promoted by the ironmaster William Reynolds. He was

43 *The Caughley saggar works, from a survey of the estate dated 1780 (SRO 1224/1/47).*

responsible for building the Hay Inclined Plane, linking the canal with the riverside and also for encouraging different industries to locate here to make best use of the land. This explains the development of Coalport in the 1790s, on a site which had previously been little more than a grassy bank (see Chapter 8).

45 *Decorative Coalport porcelain.*

44 *Gatehouse still standing at Caughley, with decorative quoins and blind windows. It was originally stuccoed. Built after 1780, perhaps to complement the elaborate Caughley Place.*

When it closed in 1926, the Coalport China Works was operated by one company, but originally the factory comprised three different potteries – an earthenware works operated between 1796 and 1800 by Walter Bradley, a porcelain works of Edward Blakeway and John Rose, in operation by 1795, and another porcelain works on the other side of the canal in existence by 1800. By 1814, the three works had been incorporated into one by the partnership of John Rose and Co.

Two eighteenth-century buildings survive; the former 'Nuway' building, and the John Rose building of 1795 (46) built by Samuel and William Smith to a design of the partners. It is a three-storey brick workshop, with multipaned windows to let as much light as possible into the manufacturing area. A range of nineteenth-century buildings survives along the river front, some of which are said to incorporate materials from the demolished Caughley Works. Most of the rest were rebuilt c.1904 by the then manager of the works, Charles Bruff,

using the same design and layout of the structures of a hundred years earlier.

Two kilns remain standing complete, and one at half height. These are typical bottle kilns – the exterior (or bottle) protected the firing operation and created a draught, while inside the pottery was stacked in saggars in a circular, roofed enclosure known as a baffle. The kilns were fired through a series of fireholes ringing the baffle. Kilns were generally short lived, being rebuilt every thirty or so years, and the surviving kilns are quite recent – the half kiln is pre-1847 and the others date to c.1910 (47).

It is not easy to say what each building was used for. Local people remember the final purpose to which each building was put – glazing in the entrance building and kiln, the two kilns to the west for biscuit firing; printing, cleaning and potting in the riverside workshops. However pottery buildings tend to be little more than generalized workshops housing processes which varied through time.

Coalport – as a known manufacturing site – has tremendous archaeological potential. Many of the buildings which existed in the eighteenth century have now been demolished, and will only be discovered through archaeology. Trial trenches have already shown that

46 *Coalport China Works at the beginning of the nineteenth century. The present John Rose building may be seen in the centre of the site* (IGMT 1986.14088).

the building to the south-east rests upon huge waste tips of pottery laid down after the floods of 1795, and similar pottery can be seen eroding out of the banks of the river to the east. The wasters from this site will enable Coalport pieces to be identified, and possibly dated, even where there is little documentation.

Creamwares

One of the most important contributions archaeology has made to the understanding of Coalport has been to re-evaluate the import-ance of Bradley's earthenware manufactory of 1796–1800. Creamware was the white-bodied earthenware manufactured by a number of firms from the mid-eighteenth century, but particularly promoted by Josiah Wedgwood at Stoke. The ware became hugely popular and filled a growing demand for tea wares and fine pottery in the home. Excavations have revealed Bradley products such as egg cups, mugs,

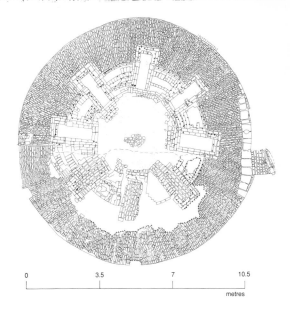

0		3.5		7		10.5

metres

47 *Coalport kiln base, now a grassed area by the present entrance building. Eight ash pits can be seen in a circle around the central oven, which was rebuilt in the nineteenth century* (IGMTAU).

sprinkler pots and teapots. Several different finishes were found including the yellowish creamware, the slightly bluer pearlware and banded wares, some of the latter finished with the distinctive mocha tree and a granite or marbled decoration. Polychrome decoration was common, as well as relief moulded Pratt wares and blue-painted and white-printed wares. Black basaltware and caneware were also made.

Creamwares, and in particular mocha wares, were also made in the potteries at Jackfield. The present Jackfield tile museum stands on top of one such pottery, where excavations revealed large quantities of mochaware and creamware wasters. Creamware wasters were also found stratified beneath an ironworking floor of 1767 at Calcutts.

There is some evidence that the manufacture of creamware was a logical development out of the earlier tradition of white salt-glazed stoneware manufacture, using the same clays at a lower temperature. This goes some way to explaining the origins of the local industry, does not explain why it remained at such a small scale.

Victorian earthenwares

The same contrast between the ornate and the mundane emerges in the pottery traditions of the nineteenth century. Plain domestic wares continued to be made at Jackfield, while other potteries produced flamboyant art pottery decorated with bunches of fruit or mirror-like lustre glazes.

John Myatt built a new pottery in Jackfield in 1836, and by 1838 was occupying the eighteenth-century earthenware manufactory, on the site of the later Jackfield tileworks. This was probably the same site as the Ivanhoe pottery where George Proudman employed 24 men and 3 boys in 1851. George Wootton took over the site in 1854, but by 1859 it was in disrepair and a new lessee was sought. The rent was £40, there was plenty of clay, coal cost 10s per ton and the works included two kilns, numerous saggars and finished yellow-brown wares and milk pans. The pottery changed hands several times, before being taken over in 1863 by John Hawes, who was joined by his son-in-law James Denny, and by 1867 they had given up pottery manufacture for encaustic tiles (see Chapter 9).

Censuses of 1851 and 1871 show that earthenware manufacture remained an important activity in Jackfield. There was a second earthenware manufactory in 1851 to the west, located in or near Exleys Brickworks at Lloyd Head, and in 1871 there were still earthenware turners and manufacturers living in the area. In 1851 Warren Taylor Jones was listed as an earthenware manufacturer and master employing six men at Benthall.

The staple products of these sites seem to have been pale yellow earthenwares, often with beaded decoration. Wasters have included large basins and pudding bowls. An inventory of moulds at the Jackfield pottery in 1860 included 'flower pots, soup tureens, dishes, jugs and teapots', a much smaller range than an earlier inventory, listing 'jugs, oval bakers moulds, beaded oval moulds, round nappies moulds, mandrin jugs, gablers, babes mugs, portland mugs, bottle moulds, coffee pot spouts and hands, and mignionette pot and stand moulds'.

The two Benthall Potteries (see p.56) remained in operation throughout the nineteenth century, united as one business in 1845. They may have still been making the brown and yellow earthenwares, but in 1845 the manager introduced 'Rockingham' wares, a rich brown glazed ware perfected at the Swinton Works.

Art pottery

In the late nineteenth century, four local ceramic firms moved towards the production of decorative art pottery, in a tradition corresponding broadly to the fashion for art castings in ironwork. The Arts and Crafts movement deplored the aesthetic and social effects of industrialization, and placed a new emphasis on craftsmanship and the role of the individual. Education was also important, and Schools of Art such as the one housed in the Literary and Scientific Institute in Coalbrookdale (see **90**), were set up for employees from the potteries, tileworks and ironworks. Designers sought to explore the full possibilities of their material – something which can be seen in the exuberant colouring and forms of Victorian art pottery.

At Benthall William Allen began making art pottery in 1882, producing moulded pieces with incised patterns. The pots were marked 'Salopian' or 'Benthall Pottery'. Surface collections from waste heaps on the Haybrook Pottery site reveal unfired teapot lids, kiln furniture and sherds of pottery which were decorated with Grecian motifs, leaves and other devices.

In 1907 the company advertised itself as the

'Benthall and Ironbridge Pottery Company, Art & Domestic Potters, glass and china merchants est. 1729'. Fragments of an unglazed 1911 coronation mug have been found at the site, as well as teapot wasters and broken candlesticks. Much of the pottery was marked by three small raised dots on the base, and has a rich brown fabric. In contrast, the waste tips on the other side of the road suggest that the Benthall site concentrated on the bulk production of more mundane items such as black glazed electrical fittings and lamp bases, coarse yellow earthenwares and thick garden pots.

The encaustic tile firms Maw & Co. and Craven Dunnill both produced art pottery for a short period, as did a firm called Woolfson Rowe and Co. which operated the Salop Pottery in the premises of the old tobacco pipe works at Benthall, from c.1922 until perhaps 1934, to be replaced by short-lived Leigh Pottery.

Conclusions

There is a vast literature on the finer pottery of the Gorge, particularly the china, and yet far less is known of the more ordinary products. The early salt-glaze industry is very apparent from archaeological remains, but is almost undocumented, and the slipwares which are so common in the area cannot be dated, and have only tenuous connections with the documented potteries. Apart from art pottery (**colour plate 11**), the nineteenth-century domestic wares are almost unknown.

Even less is known of pottery buildings – apart from the atypical Coalport, the only fragments of a pottery surviving above ground are housed in an agricultural machinery shed at Benthall. Most of the potteries have been demolished, and at least two destroyed by opencast mining.

Nowhere is the gap between the connoisseur and the archaeologist more apparent than in our understanding of the pottery of the Ironbridge Gorge; the former in the show room, concentrating on the finished pieces and their attribution, the latter in a cold finds hut, scrubbing the mud from broken bits of anonymous pottery. Both groups have much to learn from each other if we are to be able to use pottery as a primary source for understanding the past.

5

Common bricks and roofing tiles

Introduction

When a tax on bricks was proposed in 1784 there was an outcry from the ironmasters who claimed they used a million bricks a year. Bricks were essential to coal-mines – where they had replaced timber for lining tunnels; they were used also for engine buildings, in ironworking and in domestic building. In order to fulfil this demand the brick industry had undergone a transformation from a small-scale operation to one involving huge, heavily capitalized works full of machinery and capable of producing thousands of bricks and tiles each day. The industry was so successful that brick and tile production continued well after many of the other industries had closed, and Jackfield became a national centre for roof tile manufacture (48).

Brick production is one aspect of the complex process of industrialization that is poorly documented and often forgotten, due partly to a scarcity of archaeological evidence. Only one late nineteenth-century brickworks still stands and apart from the occasional chimney or shed, little remains of the many documented earlier sites. Often the only evidence available for the changing technology of brickmaking is the products themselves – either in standing buildings (colour plate 10), or scattered through the landscape in the wasteheaps around former works sites.

Buildings also provide the only evidence for the construction industry, perhaps the most elusive industry of all. Apart from notable examples such as the Iron Bridge, the individuals or firms who constructed most of the great industrial monuments have been all but forgotten, and only their work remains as witness to their achievements.

Early brickmaking

The number of brick buildings with clay-tiled roofs around the Gorge today is striking. There are only a few timber-framed cottages, and the occasional stone building or slate roof, but otherwise brick and tile are the predominant building materials in the area. Most of the buildings seen today date to the eighteenth century or later, but there is evidence for the earlier use of brick.

Brickmaking was introduced into Britain in the fifteenth century and spread gradually from the south and east, reaching the north and west later. One of the earliest brick buildings in Shropshire was Plaish Hall (1583), and bricks were first used locally in the construction of Benthall Hall (c.1583), which was fronted in stone. The octagonal tower of Willey Old Hall was the earliest building built completely of brick (49); it was already there in 1618 when John Weld acquired the estate. Other early brick buildings include Raddle Hall, Broseley (1663) and the demolished seventeenth-century Bedlam Hall. These were all examples of prestigious buildings making use of a relatively new building material; but when and how did brick and tile become the dominant building materials for buildings of all types?

Prior to the use of brick, the traditional building materials had been roughly-cut lumps of soft golden or grey Coal Measure sandstone, with thatched or tiled roofs. Many of the industrial labourers who had moved here in search of work built cottages for themselves on patches of wasteland using whatever materials they could find – stone, old bits of mine chain, rough timbers and probably coarse cloth over the windows. Very few stone cottages remain in the Gorge, although they were once common

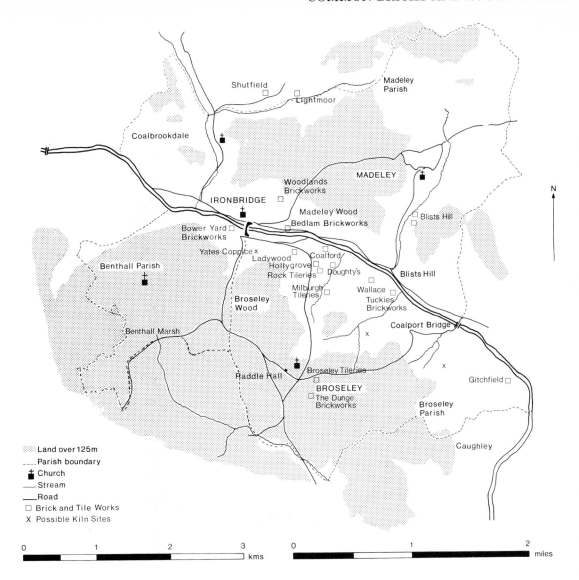

48 *Sites of brick and tile manufacture* (Judith Dobie).

in some of the older mining areas, such as Yates Coppice, located in the woods on the south side of the Iron Bridge, which, like many little communities, has now disappeared. Timber-framing was also a common building technique, sometimes in combination with stone.

Brick was first introduced as a building material for smaller houses by the landowners and entrepreneurs. Lawrence Benthall was promoting brickmaking in 1635 at Benthall Marsh where he had settled miners on former commons. His arch rival, John Weld of Willey, had an ambitious programme of building planned in 1631 and was employing a brickmaker, Jos. Whitefoot, to build cottages. Neither man was being particularly charitable – their ulterior motive was almost certainly to use the settlers to lay claim to the valuable minerals which lay under the land. Nevertheless, by building houses, they created the nucleus of several early industrialized communities. No houses remain at Benthall Marsh, but evidence from other areas suggests that the brick cottages they built were very small, with a single room downstairs and perhaps a half-attic storey above.

49 *The brick tower at Willey Old Hall, built by 1618. Note the decorative brick arcading* (Michael Worthington).

By the end of the century, more and more industrial workers were able to afford houses, and a building industry had emerged using brick and tile. Evidence for this comes from the houses, one-and-a-half-storey brick cottages, which began to appear towards the end of the seventeenth century in certain parts of the Gorge. These cottages were very different to the haphazard, self-built squatters' cottages, in that they were built to a common pattern with a degree of form and regularity which suggests that they were built by specialized builders. Many were built on old commons or land which had been sold off to tenants or speculators, and this as well as evidence from leases, suggests that ordinary people were taking responsibility for building.

Builders like Jos. Whitefoot at Willey made their own bricks. Bricks had the advantage that they could be produced on a building site using local clays, whereas stone had to be quarried or mined, cut and brought to a site

and timber was expensive and in short supply. A lease of 1734 mentions the right to make brick 'on the premises for use on the premises only', and this would have been a typical way of making brick.

An early eighteenth-century brickmaking operation would have been a very casual operation. Bricks would be moulded by hand on a table, using any of the local clays, and left to dry under a temporary shelter. Once dry, the bricks would have been stacked, covered with brush or turf and burnt in a clamp – a type of open-air firing arrangement. There would have been no permanent structures at all, and the brickmaker might have owned little more than his moulds and table, and perhaps a basic but not very effective pug mill – a barrel containing rotating knives for mixing the clay (**50**).

This description of late seventeenth-century brickmaking is reinforced by the appearance of the bricks – small and bright red, or occasionally blue and burnt, slightly bent, and containing air pockets or stones – all characteristics pointing to poor clay preparation and firing at a relatively low temperature. More elaborate technology was certainly available, and indeed commonly used in the pottery industry, but it seems that it was not worth applying to the manufacture of comparatively low value bricks.

Thus, by the beginning of the seventeenth century, brickmaking was established not in specialized brickworks, but on building sites, with individual builders/brickmakers who travelled around, responding to the needs of the wealthy landowners as well as the growing population of artisans and industrial workers.

Unfortunately, the individual builder/brickmaker was not always able to supply the needs of a large industrial enterprise. When Abraham Darby I was reconstructing the Coalbrookdale works in the early years of the eighteenth century, he obtained roof tiles from Bridgnorth and firebricks from Stourbridge, despite the fact that bricks and tiles were made locally, and suitable clays were easily available. Brick production had to be on a much larger scale if it was to cater to the demands of the ironworks and factories of the late eighteenth century.

The industrialization of brick- and tile-making

By the 1790s there were five brickworks on the south bank of the river Severn, another two on the north bank and one at Coalport. The Iron

157. BRICKFIELD, MOULDER'S BENCH, KILN, &c.

50 *An early brickworks. The clay was ground in a simple pug mill* (right) *and then moulded by hand. The example shows bricks being burnt in an open clamp, replaced in this area by kilns in the late eighteenth century* (IGMT AE 185.5668 (2)).

Bridge had been completed and the town of Ironbridge was growing fast; there were china works at Coalport and ironworks at Coalbrookdale, Bedlam, Jackfield, Barnetts Leasow, Coneybury and Benthall, all with buildings and furnaces. The population of the area was rising rapidly and people needed houses. In the coalmines – as demonstrated by the Tar Tunnel – brick had replaced timber as the material for lining shafts and tunnels. Further demand for bricks came from agriculture, which was being reorganized to supply the needs of an industrialized workforce. Many of the local farms were rebuilt at this time, with new brick barns, stabling and outhouses. Brick had become the standard material for buildings of all types. Some of this demand was supplied by specialist firms of brickmakers, and some by the ironworking companies, who as part of the process

of integrating different aspects of their activities, set up their own brickworks.

Unfortunately, not one of the documented brickworks of the 1790s survives, and the earliest map evidence of the layout for such works dates to the 1840s. It is likely that they required relatively little investment in plant and machinery, and what building there had been would have been demolished during later modernization.

However, a number of changes occur in the appearance of bricks dating to the last quarter of the eighteenth century, and these enable us to speculate about some of the differences between these brickworks and earlier ones. As before, clay would have been worked at the surface, and left to weather over the winter as the frost broke it up and made it easier to work. It would then have been prepared in a horse-driven pug mill, which would eliminate the stones and dross. Moulding was still done by hand, and drying took place in sheds with open sides. The biggest change would have been the introduction of the brick kiln, something which is suggested by the harder texture and darker colour of eighteenth-century bricks. Many of the impurities were burnt out as a result of firing at a higher temperature in a reducing atmosphere, almost certainly in a kiln. Kilns had been used in pottery manufacture since the seventeenth century, but were only adopted later in brickmaking.

The tradition of itinerant brickmaking was not totally superseded by the new works. Brick kilns were still set up where they were needed on the edges of settled areas or near the mines, and there are plenty of 'Brick Kiln' field names scattered around the area; but for the large part, big industrialized brickworks replaced the earlier temporary brickmaking sites.

The Jackfield roof tile industry

The number of brickworks continued to grow, even after other industries began to shut down. In 1840 there were at least eight factories on the Jackfield riverside alone. This is surprising, as bricks are expensive to transport and were usually made close to the site where they would

51 *Three roof tiles showing how technology changed.* From left to right: *seventeenth-century handmade tile with single nib from King Charles' Barn, Madeley; eighteenth-century handmade tile with two nibs and two peg holes, made at Exleys Works; nineteenth-century machine-made extruded tile* (Michael Worthington).

be used, yet there is no sign that local demand was expanding; most of the big ironworks had closed down, and although the town of Iron-bridge across the river was growing, there was no other large centre of population nearby to create a domestic building market. The key to the survival, and indeed growth, of these industries was the production of clay roof tiles and their export down the river to other markets – the Gorge had become a national centre for roof tile manufacture.

Roof tiles had been made here since at least 1545 when William Pinnock had a 'tylehouse' in Broseley, near the coal pits. Thick handmade roof tiles were used as an alternative to thatch on some domestic buildings, and also for industrial buildings where the thatch might catch fire. But it was in the late eighteenth century that roof tiles were made on a large scale, and even, as Arthur Young noted in 1776, exported down the river Severn to more distant markets.

Tiles were fired with bricks in the same kilns, but were made from a different clay. The clay was unique to this area, and came from a deep seam in the Middle Coal Measures. Roof tile clay could be shaped more easily, and fired to form a brown or purple coloured tile. Broseley roof tiles were famous for being extraordinarily

hard and long lasting, although they were not universally liked – in 1803 Joseph Plymley remarked rather acidly that,

> Any cover is preferable, both in look and duration to the common clay tiles of this county. Those of Jackfield indeed are durable, but all are ugly and require a sharp pitch or angle in the roof.

One source of evidence for roof tile manufacture is the characteristic 'roof-tile brick'. During firing, tiles were stacked in groups on a layer of bricks. As a result, these bricks often bear the imprint of the tile in the form of groups of five or six thin diagonal stripes. The bricks also have a dark colour, from the reducing atmosphere required for tilemaking. Roof-tile bricks provide evidence for the introduction of tile kilns – the earliest roof-tile bricks known are found in Calcutts House, dated to 1755, and such bricks become widespread in about the 1780s.

Once established the industry continued to grow, supplying a local market as well as ports further down the Severn. These early tiles are difficult to trace, as they were not always stamped (52), but the size of the works, their location on the riverside, and the link between each of the works and a riverside wharf suggests that most of their production was for export by river.

Over the next hundred years production expanded and Jackfield tiles were sold all over Britain and abroad. Advertisements in building magazines and directories lauded the quality of Broseley tiles, derived from the special, deep tile clays, and mentioned that tiles were sent to Russia, New Zealand, South and West Africa and the Gold Coast. One order was supplied to King Alphonso of Spain.

Of the ten big works on the north and south banks in 1840 mainly fragments survive – a brick-drying shed behind the Jackfield Chapel, part of a kiln fashioned out of the old Bedlam ironworks and the remains of a chimney base and sheds in what is now a metal recycling plant. The only brick-and-tileworks to stand intact is at Blists Hill, where there is a nearly complete works built by the Madeley Wood Company.

At Blists Hill, the Madeley Wood Company was still making iron and working the old coal shafts for coal and clay. This link between old coal-mines and tileworks is a common one; once

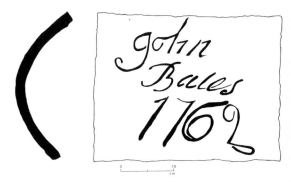

52 *Dated handmade ridge tile found at the Severn Trow, Jackfield* (IGMTAU).

the good coals were worked out, the shafts remained in use for bringing up clays and perhaps the poorer quality coals which could be used in the brick kilns. It would hardly have been worth the expense of digging shafts simply to mine low value, bulky clay.

The Blists Hill brickworks replaced an earlier one which the company had operated at Bedlam after ironworking there finished. The Bedlam works had been making white bricks from fireclay (**colour plate 10**), but at Blists Hill the works were set up to make bricks and roof tiles from the red clays and tile clays. There were two sites at Blists Hill – one on the east side of the canal, still standing, and one built later on the west side, of which only two sheds remain.

The eastern works (53) were specially built for the new plastic process introduced in the 1870s. Until then, most of the processes in brick- and tile-making were done by hand; at the new site, the clay preparation machinery was driven by steam engines, the drying sheds were specially heated with waste heat and the kilns were the more efficient down-draught types. Coal and clay were brought from the shafts across the canal and into the clay processing building, where the clay was dropped down through rollers and crushers. It was formed into slabs known as bats, and then pressed into tiles which were dried in sheds before being fired in the kilns by the canalside.

Like many of the other late nineteenth-century works, the company was producing a standard range of products, quoted in advertise-

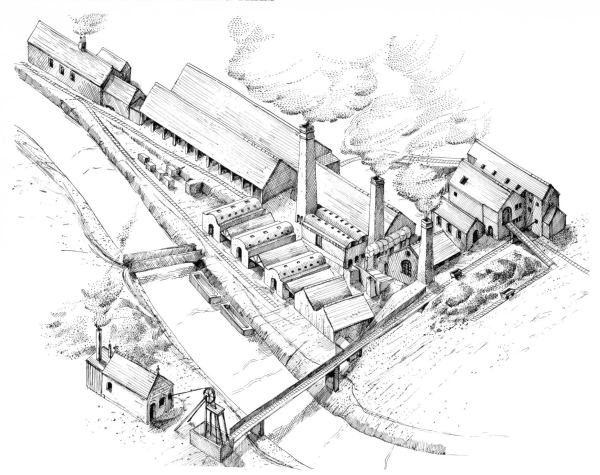

53 *Reconstruction of the brickworks on the east side of the canal at Blists Hill. Clay from the shafts was carried over the canal to weathering heaps, then taken up to the top of the clay-processing building and dropped down through grinding mills. The long buildings are drying sheds and the arched structures by the canal are kilns* (Martin Hammond/Judith Dobie).

ments as, 'Plain and ornamental pressed roof tiles, ridge hip and valley tiles in shades of red and brindled'. Some firms continued to make handmade tiles even after machinery was introduced, others made decorative ridge tiles, elaborate finials to sit on gable ends and fancy garden borders. The softer red clays were used for paviours or floor tiles, malthouse tiles and brick floors as they would wear smooth, while the white clays were used for light and coloured bricks.

The products of these brick-and-tileworks can be seen around the Gorge now – almost every house has been roofed or re-roofed in Broseley tiles, and the light bricks, such as those made at the Woodlands works, are concentrated in Ironbridge houses built from about 1800 onwards. A distinctive group of buildings of blue bricks with white brick dressings was built between about 1859 and 1862 – the bricks for at least one of these were made at the Coalbrookdale Company's brickworks. Firms constructed show-houses to demonstrate the full range of their products – the Mount House at Jackfield was built by W. Jones and The Orchard in Ironbridge, with its decorative chimneys, was built by the Davies family of brickmakers for the manager of the Craven Dunnill works.

Crisis in the industry
By 1889 the roof tile industry was coming under pressure. Other parts of the country

70

54 *Advertisement for Broseley tiles* (IGMT 1981.1604).

IMPORTANT NOTICE.

BROSELEY TILES.

IN consequence of numerous persons representing themselves as Manufacturers of the "Celebrated Broseley Roofing Tiles," we, the undersigned Firms, beg to inform the Public that we are the only Manufacturers of these Tiles at "Broseley, Shropshire"—the seam of clay from which they are made being only found at Broseley, from which place they derive their name.

BROSELEY TILERIES CO., LTD.	JONES, C. R., & SONS.
COALBROOKDALE CO., LTD.	JONES, W. & P.
DAVIS, G., SEN.	LEGGE, G., & SON.
DOUGHTY, JOHN, & SON.	MAW & CO., LTD.
EXLEY, W., & SONS.	MADELEY WOOD CO.
HAUGHTON, R. D.	PRESTAGE & CO.

55 *Advertisement placed by Broseley Tile Manufacturers Society in* The Architects Compendium and Catalogue, *1901 (IGMT).*

were producing similar tiles, and calling them 'Broseleys'. Slate was also becoming cheaper and more competitive as the railway network enabled it to be brought from Wales and distributed all over Britain. Further competition came from new roofing materials, like asbestos.

In response to these threats, the manufacturers formed an association to protect the name Broseley, claiming that the only tile that could legitimately be called a Broseley was one made from the special Broseley clay (**54, 55**). They also started applying their stamps to tiles, something which had only rarely been done before. Names such as Coalport or Sovereign Broseley make it easy to link firms to tiles, and thus to trace the distribution of tiles around Britain, but unfortunately most stamped roof tiles tend to be late in date.

To some extent all the tile manufacturers in Britain were in difficulties, but there were particular problems in this area. It was partly a matter of taste – there was an increasing demand from builders for red tiles to match the shiny red bricks then in fashion. Broseley tiles were brindled and dark, and looked dowdy when set against the new brick. When Broseley manufacturers did make red tiles, they chipped easily and were not nearly as hard as the old purple ones and Broseley tiles were beginning to lose their reputation for both strength and quality.

The sheer quantity of waste tiles from this period found heaped around Jackfield suggests that manufacturers were genuinely encountering technical problems when making red tiles. Stacks of tiles are found built into houses, used as bank retaining walls and even as garden steps. A pile of tiles, at least 5m (16½ft) high can be seen eroding into the river below the Black Swan public house and in a bank above the old railway line. Almost all of these tiles are machine made, bright red and stamped with makers' marks. Various explanations were put forward by manufacturers who laid the blame on 'bacteria' in the clay, on unscrupulous manufacturers selling underburnt tiles or on builders who put fashion before good sense.

With hindsight, it is possible to see that the technical problems might have been related to new technology. At the Blists Hill brickworks a new building was added to the old clay preparation building when the semi-plastic process was introduced in the 1890s. New machinery meant that clay could be broken down more easily and so it was possible to save time on weathering. Tiles were made much more quickly with extruding machines and the new presses, but with a disastrous loss of quality. The new process meant heavy investment in buildings and machinery at a time when the market for tiles was falling, and many firms were over-extended. Because the plant was so specialized, it was also difficult for them to diversify into other products.

Ironically, some firms found a solution in returning to the manufacture of old fashioned handmade tiles then in demand in the wake of the Arts and Crafts movement and the revival of interest in craftsmanship. In 1908 the magazine *British Clayworker* noted that the handmade, sand-faced tile was increasing in popularity, 'giving an artistic appearance to old English manor houses and country dwellings'; the Blists Hill works and others abandoned their expensive new machinery and began hand-throwing tiles again, with a genuine antique appearance.

Despite this brief revival, the market for

56 *Making roof tiles at the Milburgh Tileries, Jackfield. The kiln is in the background* (IGMT 1991.2271).

Broseley tiles declined steadily and firms began to shut down. These closures were precipitated by the labour shortages of the two World Wars. The old brickworks at the Bower Yard and the pottery at Benthall managed to survive by producing salt-glazed, stoneware sanitary pipes, but these too were forced to close by the increasing popularity of plastic drainpipes.

Brickmaking does continue today – no longer in the Gorge – but still using the same clays which made local products famous. Blockleys make bricks in Telford using Broseley clay, and on the site of the old Coalbrookdale Company works at Lightmoor, Ibstock made conservation bricks and tiles until 1991. There is now a great demand for bricks which look historic, although with electric kilns and elaborate technology, firms have yet to produce a precise match for the tough, old, handmade, coal-fired Broseley bricks and tiles.

6

Prodigious caverns and stupendous pillars of stone

The working of limestone has left huge scars in the landscape. Despite the trees which have grown up over the last few decades, it is still possible to see the great yellow gash left by quarrying on the side of Lincoln Hill, and the whole length of Benthall Edge, towering above the bridge on the other side of the river, is pitted with quarries. Until recently, it was also possible to explore a series of spectacular underground caverns, described in awe by many eighteenth-century visitors, but now filled in. These are – or were – the remains of an industry which operated for over 300 years, and which was as important as coal and iron-stone to the functioning of the iron industry.

Limestone had many uses. It was primarily used as a flux to draw off impurities from the iron during the smelting process. Burnt in a kiln with wood or coal, it formed lime which could be spread on land as a fertilizer, or alternatively used in mortar for building. Lime was also used in the household on walls as limewash, and in industries such as tanning, glass-making, bleaching and for glazing ceramics. Rough-cut limestone was a hard building stone, and crushed limestone was used as aggregate and as railway ballast.

The limestone quarries are the best preserved and most accessible of all the remains of mineral working in the Gorge. A recent study of these quarries has shown how archaeological methods can contribute to the understanding of historic landscapes, particularly when there is little documentary evidence. The surviving lime kilns are a good source of evidence for the technology of lime-burning. Neither the kilns nor the quarries should, however, be seen in isolation; like other extractive industries, they can only be understood in the wider context of

the many different activities which took place in the past (57).

The geology of limestone

A ridge of limestone crosses the Gorge from roughly north to south, and continues on towards Much Wenlock, where the ridge is better known as Wenlock Edge. To the south of the river it becomes Benthall Edge and on the north the same formation is called Lincoln Hill. Tectonic forces have in places pushed the limestone up to the surface, but to the east it lies deep beneath the Coal Measures. The limestones are part of the Silurian formation, created some 400 million years ago when the area was covered by a shallow tropical sea. Decaying coral reefs and shells settled on the sea bottom and formed the muddy shales and limestones found today. The nodules of very pure limestone found within these deposits are called 'crog balls' and are the remains of individual corals.

One of the most fascinating aspects of the Wenlock limestones is that they played a central role in the history of the science of geology. The limestone contains a sequence of small fossils which were of great interest to the nineteenth-century naturalists. The geologist Roderick Murchison was able to relate the patterns of change in the fossils to the processes which had formed the limestones, and from this to make links with other limestone formations in Britain. He named the sequence the Silurian System, after the ancient British tribe which had inhabited nearby south-eastern Wales. However, Murchison was writing in 1835, before Charles Darwin's theories of evolution had been published, and he was still constrained by the early Victorian concepts of

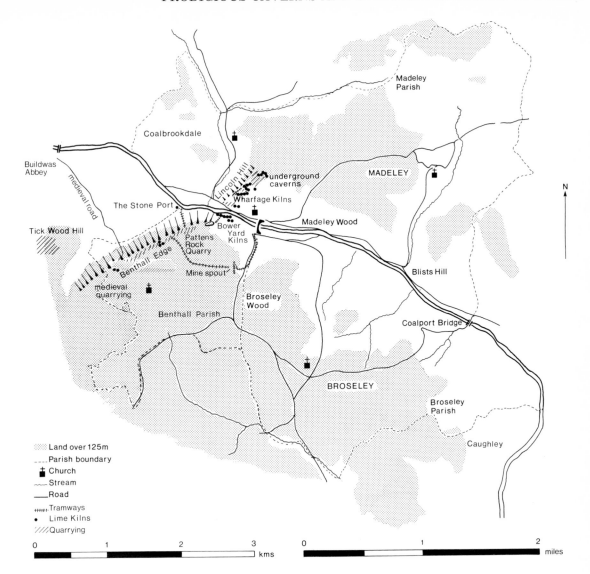

57 *Limestone formations, areas of quarrying and kiln sites* (Judith Dobie).

biblical time. He was obliged to suggest that the bedding, uplifting and erosion of the Silurian limestones were the product not of the gradual geological changes which he had observed around him, but of catastrophic events which had occurred in the relatively short period of time since Adam and Eve had been created.

His work was vindicated later and the strata which Murchison identified are still broadly accepted today, although the details have been considerably modified. This sequence is of direct relevance to archaeology, as it is imposs-

ible to read the historical landscape without understanding the geology below.

Limestone working on Benthall Edge
The analysis of a complex mining landscape is very difficult and many studies make the convenient assumption that more recent workings have destroyed all traces of earlier mining. Although this is sometimes true, the quarries of Benthall Edge have not been worked since the 1930s, and thus provide an opportunity to experiment with ways of dealing with such evidence.

Experience in excavation has given archaeologists a number of techniques for organizing

58 The Iron Bridge, *by Arthur Howe Holdsworth, with Benthall Edge towering over the bridge* (IGMT 1978.225.3).

information. The most important of these is the idea of stratigraphy – that layers on a site are deposited one after the other, and that in order to understand the site, it is necessary first to unravel this sequence of layers. The different layers are given numbers, and the relationship between all the layers is expressed in the form of a diagram or matrix. Normally this technique is confined to excavated evidence, but increasingly it is being used by archaeologists in the recording of buildings, or where there are many different changes to be analysed. At Benthall, the technique was applied to a landscape.

Benthall Edge is the high wooded scarp which towers over the south bank of the river (**58**). Along the top are a string of quarries, limekilns and associated transport links. His-

torical evidence for the quarries is scarce, and in order to learn more about them a detailed archaeological survey was undertaken. All the quarries, kilns, paths, roads, inclined planes and other features were mapped and given a number. Where possible, any pattern of changes – for example where one quarry had cut away an earlier one – was noted. The information was gathered together into a stratigraphic matrix, which produced the following broad sequence for the history of the quarries.

The earliest quarrying dated to the thirteenth century, and took place at the western end of the Edge. The quarries were linked via a medieval road to the abbey at Buildwas, where limestone was used as rubble fill for the walls and pillars, and in mortar.

During the eighteenth century the good quality limestone from the uppermost Wenlock Beds was used as a source of fluxing stone for the ironworks. It was brought down inclined planes to a point on the riverside known as the Stone Port, operated by the ironmaster William Reynolds in the late eighteenth century, and from there it was shipped across the river to Coalbrookdale or downstream to other ironworks.

In 1801 a tramway was completed, and a newspaper advertisement announced the sale of lime from the kilns at its terminus at the Mine Spout in Benthall. When limestone was burnt in kilns, the resulting lime was highly unstable and had to be kept dry; if not it could burn the hands, or react violently. As lime had to be used quickly, kilns were generally located close to where the lime was to be used. The Mine Spout kilns were supplying lime to the surrounding agricultural areas as fertilizer and to the nearby town of Benthall for building. A group of quarries can be dated to the early nineteenth century through their links with this tramway, and the exposed working faces confirm that the good stone had run out, and the lower, poorer quality Benthall Beds were being worked. There were also kilns in several of the quarries and on the riverside dating to this period.

Most of the quarries closed towards the end of the nineteenth century, although in the early twentieth century there was one final burst of activity. Patten's Rock, the limestone crag which can been seen in early engravings of the Iron Bridge, was cut away to create a huge quarry. Some of the stone was burnt for cement-

59 Tykes Nest, Broseley, *by Joseph Powell,*
c.1816–18, showing limestone quarry, railway
and the winding mechanism for an inclined
plane (Trustees of the Victoria and Albert
Museum).

making in kilns which still stand at the bottom,
and the rest crushed for aggregate. A special
siding was constructed beside the Severn Valley Railway to transport the stone away, and
the concrete piers of the aerial ropeway can
still be seen among the trees.

Taken together, the archaeological and documentary evidence enabled the four broad
phases of working to be identified – the medieval quarrying at the western end; the eighteenth-century trade in fluxing stone; the working of the poorer stones for lime in the early
nineteenth century; and finally the re-opening
of one quarry for aggregates and cements.

Limestone working on Lincoln Hill
By many accounts, the spectacular quarries,
vast caverns and the eerily lit lime kilns on the
north side of the river were far more impressive
than those of Benthall Edge. The quarries
which cut Lincoln Hill (**60**) to a sheer precipice
were as much a part of the itinerary of the
early visitor to the Gorge as the Iron Bridge or
the heat and noise of the iron furnaces at night
(**colour plate 1**).

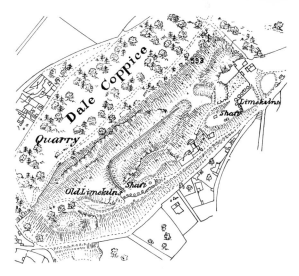

60 *Quarries and lime kilns on Lincoln Hill,*
based on the 1882 Ordnance Survey Map. In
1758 George Perry described the central quarry
as a, 'vast pit, 440 yards long and 52 wide,
each side being a frightful precipice'.

Some of the most dramatic features of Lincoln
Hill were the underground caverns, dug down
into the good quality limestone where it dipped
beneath the town of Ironbridge. According to
contemporary descriptions, great openings in
the quarry face led to the caverns, into which

just enough daylight percolated to make out the pillars and the 'grand rude arches' in the gloom. The caverns were worked on the 'pillar and stall' system, leaving columns of limestone standing to support the roof. Unfortunately, these pillars were later removed, causing the roadway above to collapse. In the interests of safety, these splendid caverns have recently been filled in and are no longer accessible. Only about a third of the caverns were explored before they were closed.

Working on Lincoln Hill broadly followed the same sequence as at Benthall Edge. The earliest reference to the mines was in 1647, when three men were killed by a fall at the lime kilns. Surface quarrying for fluxing stone took place until about 1760 and stone was supplied to the Coalbrookdale ironworks among others. The Swan public house in the Wharfage sits in one such early quarry, and in 1758 George Perry described the top of the hill as being a vast pit 440 yards long and 52 yards wide.

The caverns were dug from about 1780 onwards, once the stone which could be worked from the surface was exhausted. In 1795 the workings were bought by the Reynolds family and became part of the complex operations of the Madeley Wood Company – another example of the ironworks integrating different aspects of their business.

The accessible, good quality stone seems to have run out by 1842; the Madeley Wood Company obtained most of its limestone by canal and sold its interest in the limeworks to Edward Smith. In 1849 there were some 32 lime kilns, suggesting that there was an extensive trade in lime for building and agriculture, but in the later part of the century most extraction ceased. The quarries were briefly re-opened between 1892 and 1908 when all the old pillars were robbed out, causing the subsequent stability problems on the surface.

Lime kilns

In 1802 the painter J.M.W. Turner visited Coalbrookdale and painted a lime kiln at the foot of Lincoln Hill. In the painting the kiln is squat and sits solidly in a bare, brown landscape of quarry faces, with none of the smoke or flames which are normally so much part of our image of eighteenth-century Coalbrookdale; instead there is a sense of the bleakness and devastation of old industry. Today the kiln is barely notice-

able from the riverside as a modern house has been built close beside it.

It has been estimated that there were once 183 kilns associated with the workings on Lincoln Hill, Benthall Edge and Wenlock Edge. Today about eighty can still be identified, although most are little more than a few stones or an indentation in the ground.

All lime kilns work on the same principle – limestone is heated with charcoal or coal in order to drive off carbon dioxide and produce calcium oxide or lime. In its simplest form, a lime kiln is a cylindrical pot lined with fire-bricks. Limestone and fuel are layered in the pot, and a fire lit through the eye at the base. The eye creates a draught which keeps the fire burning and also enables the burnt lime to be drawn out through the opening. It is important to keep the finished lime dry, so the eye usually opens into a sheltered brick arch or short tunnel.

The earliest datable kilns were in use by 1800, but there are likely to be remains of earlier kilns as yet unidentified. A rough typology emerges from the kilns which have been studied – single kilns which stand isolated; paired kilns sharing a common arch (**61**), and banks of up to thirteen kilns in a row, arranged singly, in pairs or in groups of three. The sequence is not necessarily chronological – one pair of kilns was still in use in 1928, while one bank of kilns dates to 1801.

A pair of nineteenth-century kilns stands on the Wharfage, and above them the single kiln painted by Turner. On the opposite side of the river at Bower Yard is one of the best preserved kiln banks; it was built in two phases – three single kilns followed by a row of three paired kilns. The associated transport system dates the kilns to the late eighteenth century, and they went out of use about a hundred years later. The kilns were originally supplied by an inclined plane in use in 1801, which cut away an earlier zig-zag track leading to the same

61 *Reconstruction of a pair of lime kilns. The corner has been cut away to show the limestone and coal stacked in the kiln. The eye at the bottom of each kiln opens into a shared archway, which protects the burnt lime. Some form of temporary shelter would have protected the top of the kiln* (Judith Dobie).

62 *Severn trows waiting to load lime at Bower Yard lime kilns. The Severn Valley Railway, opened in 1862, is under construction (IGMT 1984.6449).*

point. The kilns were still working when the Severn Valley Railway was built in 1862, as an opening was left to allow the inclined plane to operate, and they were still in use in 1881. Between 1828 and 1863 John Patten – who gave his name to the quarry above – was a limemaster based at Bower Yard (**62**) and would have been operating the kilns.

Limestone working on Wenlock Edge

The landscapes of Benthall Edge and Lincoln Hill can be compared with Wenlock Edge to the south-west where limestone working has been more extensive, and there were originally far more kilns. The difference between the two areas is that after the Severn Valley Railway opened, working at the Wenlock Edge quarries expanded considerably and big new quarries were opened up to the south-east of the town. Since then the demand for concrete and aggregates for road building has meant that the stone has been worked continuously. Many of the old quarrying landscapes have been incorporated into huge new quarries with flat

1 *A view of Lincoln Hill with the Iron Bridge in the distance taken from the side of the River Severn*, 1788, by James Fittler (1758-1835) *(IGMT CBD 59.90.6)*.

2 *The Upper Part of Coalbrookdale*, William Westwood, published by Graf and Soret, 1835. The print shows Dale House and Rosehill House overlooking a pool just above the Coalbrookdale ironworks *(IGMT 1973.274)*.

3 *View of Bedlam Furnaces, Ironbridge,* Paul Sandby Munn, 1803
(IGMT 1986.11025).

4 *Coalbrookdale by Night,* P. J. de Loutherburg (1740-1812). An image of Bedlam
Furnaces *(Science Museum).*

5 Reconstruction of the Bedlam Furnaces *(Judith Dobie)*.

6 *Adams Engine and Ironstone Pit, Madeley Wood,* 1847, showing a Heslop Engine and beside it heaps of ironstone waste. Women were employed to pick the nodules of stone out of the clay matrix *(IGMT)*.

9 Design for a new church at Jackfield built in 1863, utilizing the many different brick colours available *(IGMT 1976.108)*.

7 Blists Hill Furnace, mid-nineteenth century. The old north engine house may still be seen on the left, and the furnaces have not yet been raised. Compare with **35** *(IGMT)*.

8 *Coalport* by H. Clements, 1884. The large warehouse straddling the canal may be seen, as well as the Coalport Bridge in the background *(IGMT 1986.9294)*.

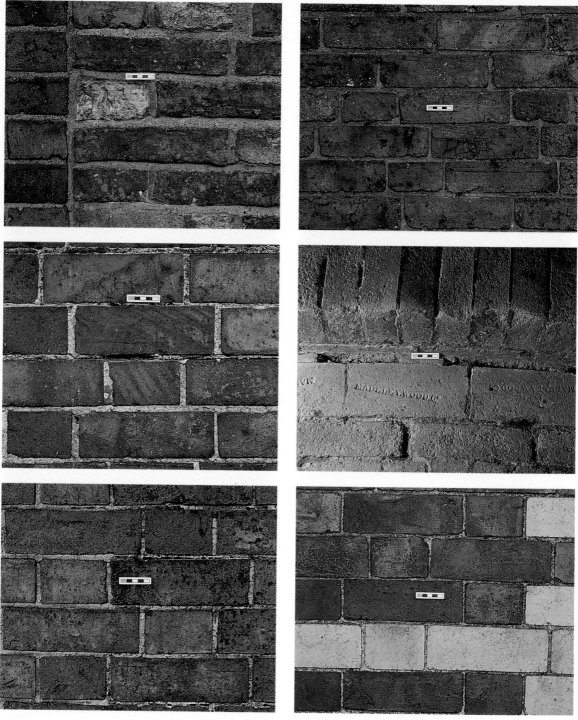

10 Brick colours:*a (Top left)* Long handmade bricks from Raddle Hall, Broseley 1663. The bricks have been washed with orange iron oxide or raddle. *b (Top right)* Handmade bricks from Calcutts House, 1755. *c (Middle left)* Roof-tile bricks from the boundary wall of Jackfield Church, 1863, although they occur in earlier buildings. *d (Middle right)* Madeley Wood Company white bricks in the steps of Ironbridge Church. They were made at the Bedlam brickworks from about 1832 onwards. *e (Bottom left)* Light coloured bricks, Ironbridge Church 1837. *f (Bottom right)* Blue and white bricks, *c.*1860, Ironbridge. *(Ben Osborne)*.

11 Art pottery vase made at Benthall
Pottery *(Michael Worthington)*.

12 Punch and Judy Tile Panel,
Maw & Co. *(1986.13866)*.

13 Reproduction medieval floor tiles, made by Craven Dunnill *(Michael Worthington)*.

14 Craven Dunnill encaustic tiles *(Michael Worthington)*.

15 Gaslit trade showroom, Jackfield Tile Museum *(IGMT)*.

floors and sheer sides, although pockets of the earlier landscape do survive in the woodlands owned by the National Trust.

Quarries are not normally seen as important archaeological sites and in the study of the limestone industry far more attention is paid to kilns. Yet without their surrounding landscape, lime kilns are relatively uninformative. The tramways, kilns, spoil heaps, quarries and inclined planes of Benthall Edge represent a complete landscape, free from the ravages of modern quarrying and of great value both in archaeological terms and as attractive scenery. The beauty of Wenlock Edge has attracted the attention of musicians and poets, and is still seen as a landscape of national value, yet it also has an historical dimension, which could easily be eroded without proper care.

Careful fieldwork has demonstrated the potential contribution of mining landscapes to historical knowledge. This raises an important conservation issue – in order to understand the landscape it is necessary to study not one but all of the quarries with their associated features. This therefore demonstrates the need for preserving entire landscapes rather than single quarries or isolated kilns.

7

The Iron Bridge

The elegant arch of the Iron Bridge, rising above the river between the steep sides of the Gorge, has become a symbol for the whole area. Since it opened to traffic in 1781 it has attracted countless visitors from all over the world, who marvel at its technical ingenuity, its setting and its significance. It gave its name to the local town and has spawned imitations in Britain and abroad. It remains today an icon of Britain's industrial achievement in the eighteenth century (colour plate 1).

But the bridge is more than just a feat of engineering. It made a huge impact on the history of art in Britain, attracting major artists to industrial rather than classical landscapes; it represents a triumph for its promoters, who had hoped that it would allay suspicions about the strength of iron. It transformed the surrounding landscape, altering the pattern of roads and settlement and the way goods were able to move about the Gorge. Much has been, and will continue to be, written about the bridge and here it is possible only to introduce a complex and fascinating subject.

Who built the bridge?

Until the 1770s, the only means of crossing the river Severn was via the old medieval Buildwas Bridge, 4km (2.5 miles) to the west, or on one of the ferry boats which plied back and forth across the river (63). As early as 1773 a plan was put forward to construct a new bridge. In 1776 a group of subscribers, including Abraham Darby III, put a petition before parliament for a new bridge, claiming that,

> ...a very considerable traffic is carried on at Coalbrookdale, Madeley Wood, Benthall, Broseley &c. in iron, lime, Potters clay and coals, and persons carrying on the same frequently are put to great inconveniences, delays and obstructions by reason of the insufficiency of the present ferry over the River Severn .... particularly in the Winter.

One of the people involved was Thomas Farnolls Pritchard, a Shrewsbury architect who had undertaken several other bridge projects (64). In 1773 he wrote to the ironmaster John Wilkinson, suggesting that an iron bridge should be constructed across the river. He later submitted a design for an iron bridge, much wider and shallower than the present bridge, which the Trustees accepted. Abraham Darby III was commissioned to build the bridge (65).

Although the petition to parliament was successful, there were strong doubts about the feasibility of a cast-iron bridge. Authority was given to build a bridge in 'cast iron, stone, brick or timber' and this reflected the dissent which had arisen amongst the Trustees about whether cast iron was, after all, a suitable material. Masonry was the most common choice of building material for bridges, and although slow to build and costly, stone bridges had been proved to be strong and durable. Iron was beginning to be used as a building material in architecture, mainly to strengthen existing construction, but it had never been used for a bridge. Only after several months of arguing did the bridge Trustees finally agree to build in cast iron, but it was made very clear that the financial risk should fall upon Abraham Darby III himself.

When work began in 1777, it was to a design for a bridge that was rather different to Pritchard's original drawing. Pritchard died in that year without leaving any other designs. Yet

63 (Above) *View of the Gorge before the bridge was built, painted by William Williams, 1777. The Iron Bridge was built at a point just beyond the three boats on the south* (left) *bank* (IGMT 1985.197).

64 (Left) *Thomas Farnolls Pritchard (1723–77), credited with the design of the Iron Bridge* (IGMT 1978.218).

it is clear from looking at the bridge, from Pritchard's earlier involvement, and from elements of Pritchard's other works which use the same motif of a circle and ogee, that he was the prime instigator. It has now largely been accepted that it was indeed Thomas Farnolls Pritchard who provided the design for the Iron Bridge (**66**).

The construction of the bridge

The location chosen was that of the ferry-crossing from Benthall to the bottom of Madeley Wood. At first sight it seems to have had few advantages. It was some distance away from existing turnpikes so that new roads

65 The Iron Bridge from Lincoln Hill, *George Robertson (1724–88) (IGMT AE 185.765).*

would have to be built and local tracks upgraded. Access down the sides of the Gorge would be difficult and it was not particularly close to any of the major ironworks. Yet the approaches to the bridge on both sides were high, which would avoid the need for big earthworks on either side of the river, the site is away from the major areas of landslip to the east, and, in comparison to the banks up and down stream, relatively stable. Another factor in choosing the site may have been the pattern of land ownership – the Benthall ferry and southern approach were owned by one of the subscribers to the bridge, who stood to gain considerable commercial advantage from the project.

A surviving estimate for the building of the bridge gives some idea of what was involved –

300 tons of cast and wrought iron were needed, produced either by the up-grading of the Coalbrookdale furnace or alternatively from the Madeley Wood Company furnaces at Bedlam. The bridge itself consists of five cast-iron segmental frameworks, each of which is braced to two inner part ribs. Most of the joints resemble traditional timber joints – dowels, mortices and half laps – reflecting a greater confidence in the tried techniques of timber construction than in the new cast iron. The actual ironwork may well have been cast on or near the site of the bridge from temporary re-melting furnaces, although no archaeological evidence for this has yet been found.

66 *'Design for a Cast Iron Bridge between Madeley and Broseley by F.Pritchard, 1765', published posthumously by John White in 1835. The final design incorporated elements of each of these sketches* (IGMT 1986.8609).

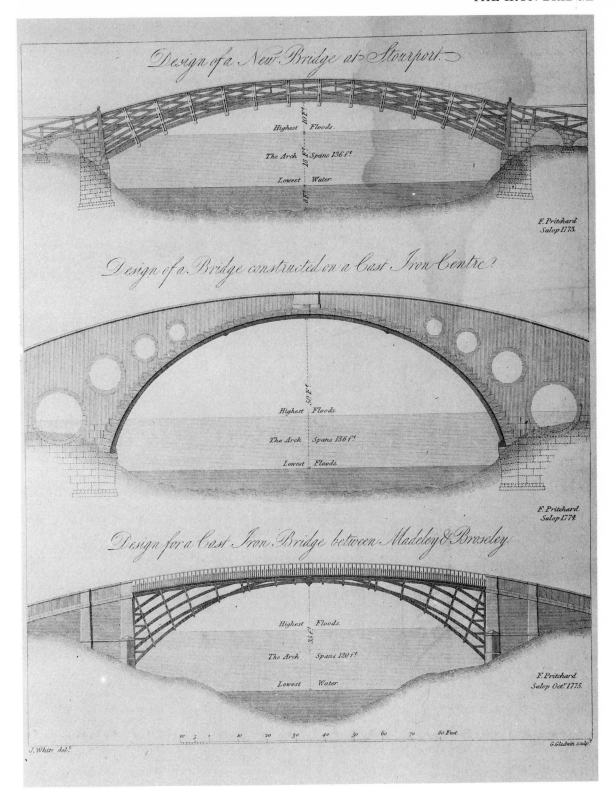

Design of a New Bridge at Stourport.

Highest Floods.

10 F.t

18 F.t

The Arch Spans 136 f.t

Lowest Water.

9 F.t

F. Pritchard.
Salop 1773.

Design of a Bridge constructed on a Cast Iron Centre.

50 F.t

Highest Floods.

The Arch Spans 136 f.t

Lowest Floods.

F. Pritchard.
Salop 1774.

Design for a Cast Iron Bridge between Madeley & Broseley.

Highest Floods.

36 f.t

The Arch Spans 120 f.t

Lowest Water.

F. Pritchard
Salop Oct.r 1775.

10 5   10   20   30   40   50   60   70   80 Feet.

J. White del.t

G. Gladwin sculp.t

A separate estimate was given for the decorative ironwork for the railings and parapets, which must have included the fine roundels in the centre of the bridge. Early pictures show that several lamps were intended, although more accurate engravings show only a central lamp.

The bridge was carried between two huge stone abutments filled with rubble and faced with fine stone ashlar. Brick was becoming an increasingly popular building material, but eighteenth-century brick was not strong or water resistant, and stone was always used for retaining walls and damp areas. Brick was used for the vault of the side arch on the north side behind the ashlar facing.

The estimate indicates that 600 yards of digging and clearing on either side of the river were needed in order to set the abutments on to solid bedrock below the covering of topsoil and loose material. In fact, the later problems with the south abutment seem to have been caused by insufficient care during this part of the works. An item for gravelling is mentioned, perhaps for access roads, working areas around the bridge or the surface of the bridge itself.

Timber for scaffolding was a large item of expenditure and provisions for carrying the proprietor's timber were established in the original agreements. It has been suggested that in order to get the members into place, two wooden towers were built in the river leaving a clear space between to allow navigation to continue. The iron members were then lifted into position from a crane on the tower and set into the partly completed abutments.

Finally, the estimate included the costs of making drawings and other incidentals (possibly payments to Thomas Farnolls Pritchard as designer) and items for the construction of approach roads.

In the event, expenditure far outweighed the original estimate of £3250. Problems with roads in particular had pushed up the costs to something closer to £5000, much of which was borne by the Coalbrookdale Company and by Abraham Darby III himself, who remained in debt for the rest of his life.

Cast iron as a building material

Perhaps Darby's enthusiasm was fuelled by an inkling of how important the bridge might be as an advertisement for the properties of cast iron. There is no doubt that the initial significance of the bridge was to demonstrate to the engineering profession that cast iron could be successfully used as a construction material. Hitherto, iron had been used in a limited fashion, in conjunction with timber or masonry. By building an arch completely of iron, Darby and his partners were able to demonstrate basic principles of cast-iron construction which many others were to copy.

Imitations of the new bridge soon followed – in the 1780s small ornamental iron bridges were built near Paris at Raincy and at Worlitz in Prussia. Another iron bridge was cast at Coalbrookdale in 1794 for the Marquis of Stafford and used at Trentham. Confidence grew, particularly after the disastrous Severn floods of 1795 when the Iron Bridge was the only one of the bridges on the river to remain undamaged, and also after the construction of an even larger iron bridge at Sunderland which spanned a greater length than would have been possible in masonry. In the Gorge, Thomas Telford replaced the medieval bridge at Buildwas with a new bridge of iron in 1795–6 (**67** and see **7**). North of the Gorge is Telford's Longdon-on-Tern aqueduct of 1796; lighter and stronger than traditional aqueducts it perhaps saw the first use of iron in beam construction.

Cast iron was brittle, and although strong under compression it was weak in tension. The next major development was the introduction of the more elastic wrought iron in bridges, such as the suspension bridge built by Telford over the Menai Strait. Nevertheless, one of the advantages of cast iron was that the pieces could be fabricated at the ironworks and transported to the bridge site. Even after the introduction of wrought iron, cast iron continued to be used, often for railway bridges which were some distance from sources of iron. Unfortunately the weakness of cast iron in tension resulted in the failure of a girder bridge and this, followed by the collapse of the Tay Bridge in 1879, marked a clear loss of confidence in cast iron. Wrought iron continued to be used, but after the construction of the Forth Bridge in 1890, mild steel became the accepted medium. In 1878 one of the last bridges to use cast iron was built carrying the Great Northern Railway across Friargate in Derby.

Changes to the Iron Bridge

The Iron Bridge as seen today is not as it was built – the iron arches are largely the same,

67 Buildwas Bridge, Colebrook Dale, *Arthur Howe Holdsworth* (1780–1860). *Pen, ink and wash drawing of the iron bridge designed by Thomas Telford to replace the medieval one, damaged in the 1795 flood. It was demolished in 1905, though the abutments still stand* (IGMT 1978.225.4).

but changes have taken place in the abutments, approaches and structure (**68**).

The biggest change has been to the south abutment. Analysis of early pictures shows that the original construction involved a solid stone abutment on the south side, similar to, but much larger than, that on the north. Problems with the bridge were already apparent in 1791–2; the south abutment had cracked due to subsidence and had to be repaired. Although the bridge survived the 1795 floods which destroyed many other bridges, the abutment cracked again in 1801 and was demolished. Two new stone piers were built with a wooden roadway between them. The wooden supports were finally replaced in 1820–3 by the iron

arches, which can be seen today on the south side. Repairs to these two small spans took place in 1845, the 1860s, 1879 and 1911.

Alterations have also taken place to the north abutment since the original bridge was built. In 1782 Richard Reynolds was allowed to take down the parapet walls and the foot of the bridge on the Madeley side in order to accommodate a building, and eleven years later his son was authorized to take down part of the west wall. This may in part have related to the construction of the Tontine stables close to the west abutment.

One of the continuing causes of concern to engineers has been the strength of the cast-iron structure. The bridge remained in full use for over 150 years – first by the carts bringing industrial goods across the river, followed by long distance stage-coaches which were diverted across the new bridge. From 1862 it became the only link between the town of Iron-bridge and the new railway station on the south bank, and despite the opening of the Free Bridge in 1909, it was used by more and more vehicular traffic. There was general concern about the ability of the bridge to carry such

THE IRON BRIDGE

a *IRON BRIDGE AS BUILT 1779*

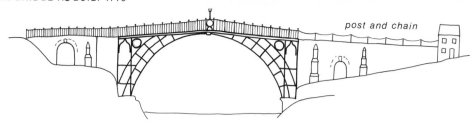
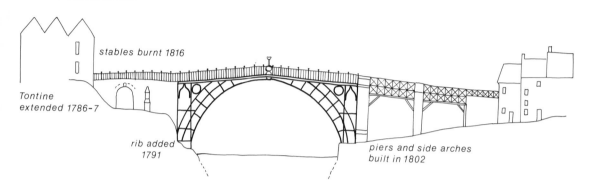

post and chain

b *IRON BRIDGE 1804*

stables burnt 1816

*Tontine
extended 1786-7*

*rib added
1791*

*piers and side arches
built in 1802*

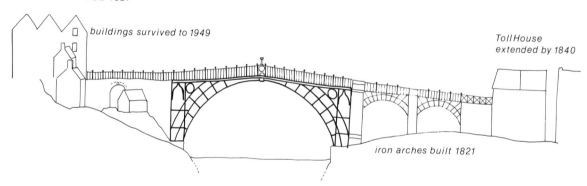

c *IRON BRIDGE 1821*

buildings survived to 1949

*Toll House
extended by 1840*

iron arches built 1821

d *IRON BRIDGE 1950*

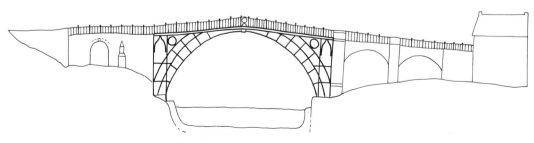

coffer dam built 72-4

traffic, and in the 1920s there was talk of demolishing the bridge and replacing it with a modern concrete structure to service the new power station. It was only in 1934, when it was designated as an Ancient Monument, that the bridge was finally closed to vehicular traffic.

Since then engineers have been monitoring the bridge to assess its stability. A report on the condition in 1902 revealed fractures to the ribs, and was followed by some repairs. In 1923 the thickness of the roadway was reduced, and footpaths added to relieve loading. The problem was such that by 1969 the abutments had moved towards each other by 48cm (19in), creating stresses on the cast iron; cracks in the arch had first been noted in 1784, and there was some debate as to how significant they were. Several solutions were suggested, including lifting the bridge and placing it on bearings to allow it to move. It was finally decided to build a concrete strut under the arch in the river to hold the abutments apart in 1972–3; a similar solution had been tried, and failed, in 1801. Some of the fill was also emptied from the north abutment to allow concrete strengthening to be inserted (69). The roadway was renewed in 1974 and in 1980 there were further repairs to the ironwork and the whole bridge was repainted.

The infrastructure of the Iron Bridge.
It was not just the bridge which caused problems for the proprietors. Having built the bridge, they then turned their attention to the road network.

68 *Changes to the Iron Bridge:*

a. *The bridge as built in 1779. The south abutment is stone and part of one rib is missing.*
b. *The bridge in 1804. The south abutment (right) has been replaced by a timber deck. The tollhouse has been extended and the Tontine hotel extension built on the north side in 1786–7. The Tontine stables on the far side were burnt down in 1816.*
c. *The bridge after 1821. Iron arches have been built to the north, and the tollhouse was extended by 1840.*
d. *The bridge today. The Tontine building and the one by the tollhouse have been demolished, and a coffer dam built under the bridge in 1972–4 (David de Haan/Judith Dobie).*

The road to the south of the bridge runs steeply up the hill towards Benthall. Before the bridge was built it had been the line of an old plateway, but it was given to the proprietors of the bridge in exchange for free maintenance. There then followed a catalogue of troubles caused by local industrialists, the steep slope of the road as well as poor drainage caused by a geological fault which runs across the road. The road was repaired with ash and cinders from the local furnaces, probably using the recipe cited in the minutes of the proprietors' meetings: '3 tons of furnaces cinders to each yard in length of a road nine yards wide, with 30 loads of ashes to cover them'.

Despite building soughs and drains, water continued to run down the road making it impassable. The ironworks dumped cinders, ashes and other obstructions on the road and Serjeant Roden was told not to unload and leave any limestone there. Attempts were made to widen the road; potters' ovens and pig-sties were taken down to do this, and posts and rails were put up along the road to make it safer. Finally, in 1828, the struggle was abandoned, and a new road built up to Broseley.

Transport to the north was even more of a problem. No roads led to the new bridge site, so the proprietors were obliged to use the Coalbrookdale Company private road along the Wharfage. Not only did they have to pay the company, but they had to resurface the road and build stone walls to prevent it slipping into the river. These walls can still be seen today along the Wharfage riverside, and were built by stonemason Edward Nicholls, who charged '5s each square yard and 5s over', and undertook to obtain and transport the stone himself. The road remained in the hands of the Coalbrookdale Company until 1806 when the road was turnpiked.

From the Wharfage it was still difficult to reach the turnpike roads at the top of the hill, so in 1810 Madeley Hill was constructed, an extraordinary piece of road engineering, cutting up the hill towards Madeley and supported on brick arches.

The image of the Iron Bridge
The view of the Iron Bridge is firmly implanted today as a symbol of the Industrial Revolution. It is used constantly in books, souvenirs and on television in Britain and abroad, and has become one of the best known images of indus-

Excavated north abutment

Concrete invert arch

69 *Diagram showing the repairs undertaken to the Iron Bridge in 1973* (IGMT 1981.657).

trialization. This success is the culmination of a long tradition of deliberate promotion of the Iron Bridge.

The image of the Iron Bridge owes its popularity to some of the most famous artists of the eighteenth, nineteenth and twentieth centuries. J.M.W. Turner, Philip James de Loutherburg, John Sell Cotman, and more recently John Nash and John Piper all found subject material in the Gorge, its bridge and its industries. In the eighteenth century these images were some of the earliest examples of industrial art and did much to create the popular impression of industry as both sublime and horrific. Artists were beginning to move away from classical motifs towards new and more dramatic themes. At least fifty artists painted the area between 1750 and 1830, and some thirty original paintings or drawings have been traced. From these, countless engravings and reproductions were made.

In choosing the site for the Iron Bridge the promoters were aware of the dramatic qualities of the Gorge and the effect of a bridge sited directly between the towering hills on either side. Views of the bridge were being advertised in the *Shrewsbury Chronicle* in June 1780, even before the bridge had been completed. Abraham Darby III commissioned one of the first views of the bridge from William Williams, who was paid 10 guineas in 1780 for drawing a view of the bridge. He showed it from the east, against a stormy sky, with busy scenes of industry in the background and an elegant group of tourists in the foreground, observing the bridge from a boat. In January 1781 Darby paid a fee and travelling expenses to Michael Angelo Rooker, the scene painter at the Haymarket Theatre, for a view of the bridge, which was reproduced over and over again by the engraver William Ellis (**70**) and distributed through London book-

70 (Above, right) The Cast Iron Bridge near Coalbrookdale, 1782, *engraving published by William Ellis after Michael Angelo Rooker (1743–1801)* and commissioned by Abraham Darby III *(IGMT 1983.1333).*

71 (Below, right) Elevation and detail of the Ribs of the Iron Bridge ..., 1782. *Engraving by William Ellis after Michael Angelo Rooker (1743–1801). Given to subscribers with the general view of the bridge by the same artist* (see **70**) (IGMT SSMT 43).

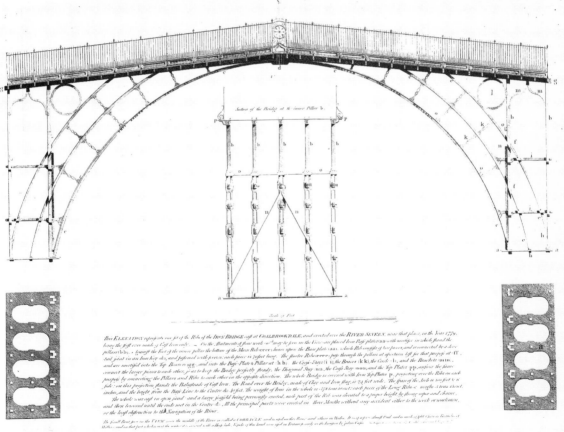

sellers. In Rooker's picture, the bridge is a little further away and the hills on both sides can be clearly seen. Traffic is crossing the bridge, the figures dwarfed by the exaggerated railings. There is a suspicion that neither of these artists actually saw the bridge completed and were working from engineering drawings as their pictures leave out details which had not been built at the time.

Set against the aesthetic impact of the bridge was a sense of wonder at its technical achievement. Purchasers of Ellis's engraving were given a free gift of a measured elevation of the bridge with a description of its construction (71). From then on, most of the published engravings included at least the dimensions of the bridge and a brief account of its construction, suggesting that it was the technical achievement of the bridge as much as the view which attracted buyers. Many of the major engineers and entrepreneurs of the eighteenth century had some connection with the Gorge. Thomas Telford, William Jessop, John Rennie, Benjamin Outram, Richard Trevithick, John Curr, James Watt, Matthew Boulton and John Loudon McAdam all knew of and were associated with developments here. For engineers, the bridge remained a symbol of the historic achievements of their profession, and visits by professional groups such as the Iron and Steel Institute continued during the late nineteenth century, when the popularity of the Gorge was at a low ebb. It was an article in *The Engineer* which spoke out when the Iron Bridge was threatened with demolition in 1926 (see p.124).

Engravings of the bridge were not the only means by which images reached households around the country. Using the newly available techniques of transfer printing, pictures of the bridge appeared on commemorative mugs and plates produced by the Caughley and Coalport porcelain manufacturers (72). Local shopkeepers and manufacturers used the bridge on letterheads, but it was the Coalbrookdale company which made most use of the image. Tokens were struck, using the bridge on the reverse. Fire grates – one of their most widely sold items – were cast in the shape of the arch. A whole range of other objects appeared with the bridge displayed on them, including brooches (73), snuff boxes and handkerchiefs.

The bridge continued to attract artists in the early nineteenth century, and indeed until well into this century when both John Nash and John Piper painted it. The late nineteenth century, however, was the first age of the photographer, and a vast collection of photographs housed in the Ironbridge Gorge Museum Trust's Library demonstrate the interest generated by the area. Many of these images were reproduced as postcards to be sold to visitors.

Through constant use and repetition, the image of the bridge had become a popular symbol of the Industrial Revolution – what had initially been the subject for polite art, pictures painted for the drawing rooms of discerning gentlemen, had spread to reach a much wider audience.

The bridge today

The bridge was closed to vehicles in 1934 but it remained open to foot passengers. In 1950, ownership was transferred to Shropshire County Council and the bridge then came under the guardianship of what was to become English Heritage. Since then, the town of Ironbridge was included in the Telford Development Corporation and became the focus of the Severn Gorge Conservation area. The whole area was designated a World Heritage site in November 1986.

Many of the changes that have since taken place result from the need to cater for increasing numbers of visitors, and are a reflection of conservation requirements as well as civic pride. The building which had originally served as the Toll House was reopened as an information centre relating to the bridge in 1971. Across from this another small brick building, held together with iron ties, which once formed part of the gate arrangement, lies derelict.

Apart from repairs, other changes have taken place around the bridge in recent years. On the north bank, the flower beds to the east and west were once the site of buildings which towered over the bridge, crowding the approach with shops and other activities. These areas have now been opened out and landscaped with

72 (Above, right) *Coalport cup, showing the Iron Bridge from the east. The Tontine stables are still standing on the north bank on the site of the modern viewing platform* (IGMT).

73 (Below, right) *Ladies brooch, showing the Iron Bridge* (IGMT).

74 *Cast-iron roundel erected on railings overlooking the bridge* (Michael Worthington).

new walls and railings. The market place has been remodelled, and the war memorial which was once on the corner moved across to the side of the bridge and set in a small seating area. On the south side, the old railway station stood in what is now the car-park; it was demolished and only the rails remain where the level crossing once was.

The bridge today is very different even to the bridge of fifty years ago, and there is no doubt that public interest in it is growing. In 1988 almost 800,000 people came to the area, half of whom came just to look at the bridge. If nothing else, this is a vindication of the confidence and faith of Abraham Darby III and his partners in building the first iron bridge.

8

Roads, railways, canals and inclines

The Iron Bridge was a bold and innovative solution to a long-established problem – getting down to, and across, the Gorge. The steep sides drop over 100m (329ft) to the river with a gradient that sometimes approaches one in one. Added to this the slopes are unstable, slipping constantly as the river erodes a course through the geologically young valley. There are few potential bridge sites, and those that do exist have other drawbacks. Getting bulky raw materials such as coal down to the riverside and across the river required ingenuity.

Once down on the riverside, the next transportation hurdle was the river Severn itself. Prior to the eighteenth century rivers were the main highways of Britain, and the Severn was no exception, creating a link between the coalfields, Bristol and the sea. The river was one of the primary attractions of the Gorge but despite many attempts by industrialists, it was never improved and remained unreliable. In winter, floods lapped over the sides of the wharfage walls and damaged bridges; in summer it was often impassably low for boats of any size.

The ability to move goods around, and to bring them in and out, was vital to any industrial operation (75). For hundreds of years, industrialists wrestled with the problems of transport the Gorge created, producing daring solutions that were often applied to other parts of Britain. Few of their efforts lasted long, and eventually the area became once again the backwater that it had been in the medieval period.

The early railway network
Most of the medieval roads of any consequence bypassed the Gorge; the only bridge was at Buildwas, 4km (2.5 miles) to the west (see 7),

and the only other means of crossing the river would have been shallow fords. The Gorge was a wooded, isolated valley with few links with the outside world, apart from the river.

It was not until the growth in coal-mining in the sixteenth and seventeenth centuries that the need to open up the area became imperative. Although the Severn provided an ideal means of getting coal to markets, the problem was getting the coal to the river. Coal was bulky and the cost of loading individual packhorses to carry it down muddy tracks must have been prohibitive. The solution was the use of some of the first railways – or waggonways as they are sometimes known – in Britain. In order to overcome the problem of horse-drawn carts becoming bogged down, wooden rails were laid along the tracks. The carts – or waggons – were fitted with flanged wheels which would keep them on the rails. These were the predecessors of modern railways, and were in use in coal-mining areas long before even canals were common.

The first known waggonways in the country were used at Newcastle, but shortly afterwards, in 1608, court records suggest that they were in use here. James Clifford, who owned much of Broseley, was in dispute with his tenant, Richard Willcox, over his coal mines. The case makes wonderful reading; it seems railways aroused as much passion then as they do today. Apparently, Willcox had erected a 'vary artificiall Engine or Instruments of timber', to get coal down to the riverside which had cost him over two hundred marks (about £140). The engine was moved by one man, and could move more in a day than a 'wayne with six oxen', could in three or four. It sounds like an arrangement shown in later illustrations, with a man

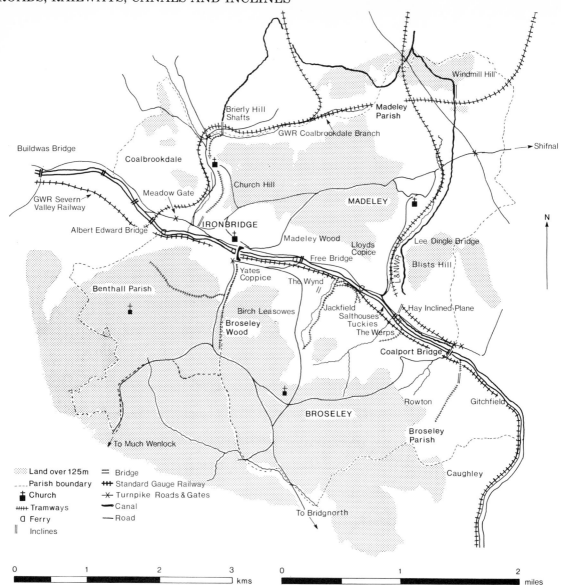

Land over 125m
Parish boundary
Church
Tramways
Ferry
Inclines
Bridge
Standard Gauge Railway
Turnpike Roads & Gates
Canal
Road

75 *Map of transport-related sites* (Judith Dobie).

sitting on a waggon running downhill on a waggonway, using a brake lever for control. Clifford was accused of damaging the railway, but he denied this and retorted that Willcox was simply trying to extract compensation. Whatever the justice of the issue, the point was that the documents suggest that railways were being used here already.

These first lines were very short, but by the end of the century there is good evidence for much longer lines of up to 1400m (1500yds). It is not easy to find field evidence for these early routes. Even where the route can be identified from documents, there may be nothing on the ground. Any one of the historic routes down the hill from Broseley could have been used by Richard Willcox. One of the problems is that the routes were ephemeral, and lines were often taken up after they went out of use – one line was once described as being of the 'mushroom breed, the product of a single night'. Fieldwalking over ploughed land at Rowton, for example, revealed nothing of the railway which crossed it – not even a dark stain from the ash which

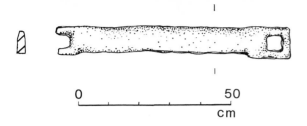

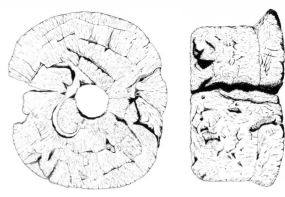

76 *Part of an early Coalbrookdale rail, found at Newdale* (Shelley White).

lined the track, or a faint depression from wear. Part of the reason for this is that early waggonways did not involve the level of engineering of later routes. Rather than construct earthworks to keep lines level, they often snaked up and over hills, or took longer routes to follow contours.

One wooden waggonway wheel has been found from Broseley (**77**), and parts of an intact wooden waggonway were found near Bedlam Furnaces in 1986 (**78**). The rails were of heavily worn oak, and were pegged on to sleepers and set on a bed of slag. The gauge was 3ft 9in (115cm) and the sleepers were set 2ft 4in (69cm) apart. This waggonway was rather later, dating to 1750–60, by which stage cast-iron wheels had probably been adopted for the waggons.

Horse-drawn waggonways remained in use until the nineteenth century, particularly for transporting goods around local sites. Some of the later routes, however, were more sophisticated, with level tracks and embankments carrying lines around hillsides. One waggonway bridge survives at Newdale, to the north of the Gorge, where an arched stone bridge of *c*.1759 carried a line across a stream towards the Horsehay ironworks. The bridge represents a permanent investment in a line by an iron-working company, in comparison to the earlier, temporary routes.

Iron bars from excavations nearby have just been identified as examples of the next major change in railway technology – the adoption of iron rails (**79**). Iron wheels and axles had been in use since 1726, but by 1767 Richard Ford of the Coalbrookdale Company claimed that they were using iron rails. Two pieces of iron, found reused in a window frame of 1768, proved to be examples of the earliest iron rails (see **76**). They had been broken in half, but

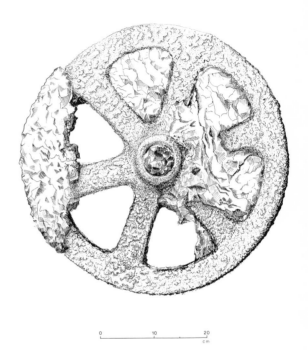

77 *Wooden waggonway wheel and iron plateway wheel* (John Moore/Susan Isaac).

originally consisted of single rails, 140cm (55in) long, 7.5cm (3in) wide and 2cm (1in) thick, with holes at either end and in the middle to attach them to wooden rails below. Such rails sat upon wooden bases, replacing the oak upper rails which had been used earlier. It is possible that the Bedlam rails may even have been wooden bases for this type of upper rail. The Newdale rails were the first example of Coalbrookdale rails ever to have been found.

Much more common are the later 'L'-shaped iron rails known as plateways, on which a

97

78 *The wooden waggonway found by Bedlam Furnaces. The wood might have been a base for cast-iron rails (IGMTAU).*

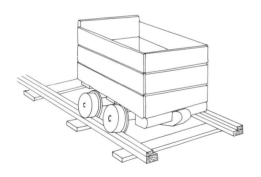

a

b

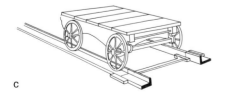

c

79 *Early railways (approx. scale 1:40):*
a. Wooden waggonway with flanged wheels in use by 1608.
b. Iron rails laid on wooden bases, introduced 1767.
c. L-shaped plateway invented by John Curr and in use by 1790s (Shelley White).

waggon with unflanged wheels would have run. A huge collection of such rails has been found from all over the Gorge; many have the names of the firm cast in them, and many are special shapes for junctions or corners. They were used throughout the nineteenth century for transporting goods between different parts of a works, or for building up the huge spoil heaps of slag and waste.

Plateways remained in use as a local network even after the construction of standard gauge railways. The Lee Dingle plateway bridge at Blists Hill, for example, was built by the London and North Western Railway (L&NWR) company in 1859 so that the brickworks could continue to use local plateways to bring coal from nearby pits. The bridge caused a huge amount of controversy between the British Transport Commission and the brickworks; after the mainline went out of use, the commission wanted to demolish the bridge and so removed the timbers. The brickmakers were furious and demanded compensation, and when this was refused tried to give the steel superstructure to the Lilleshall Company in settlement of a debt. Finally, the brickmakers refused to let the bridge be demolished until the commission cleaned up the canal, which they refused to do. Fortunately the bridge is still there, a fine listed monument, towering over the Blists Hill valley.

The Lee Dingle Bridge and the plateway/railway interchange below it where goods from the plateway network could be transferred on to main lines, were some of the last examples of engineering associated with the local railway network which had spread across the Gorge, the end of a tradition which had originated in the early 1600s.

'Winds' and 'tylting rails'

In addition to getting around the Gorge, there was the problem of getting down the steep slopes. In order to move coal down to the waiting boats, early railway builders adopted an ingenious solution – the 'wind'.

Two years after their first dispute, James Clifford and his tenant Willcox were back in the Star Chamber of James I. This time, Willcox and his partner Wells had taken revenge

80 Reconstruction of the Hay Inclined Plane, Coalport. From the canal at the top, tub boats were floated on to cradles. These were wound down the rails to a stretch of canal at the bottom running parallel to the river. Goods were trans-shipped into trows using one of seven small inclines between the canal and river. A large warehouse spanned the canal (Shelley White/Judith Dobie).

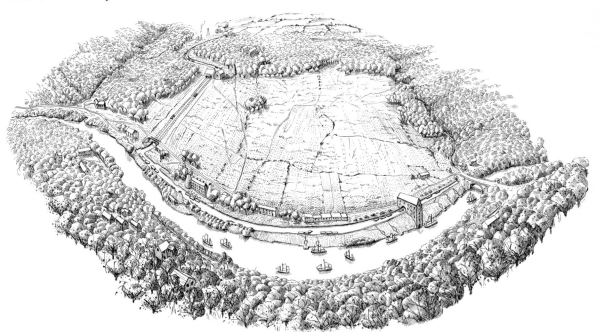

against Clifford by demolishing a set of 'tylting Railes', and cutting the ropes by which Thomas Presscott carried coals from a pit to the river Severn for James Clifford.

This arrangement has been interpreted as a short inclined plane where a winding drum at the top let a waggon down the hill on a pair of rails. They were fairly common, and one little cottage at Jackfield on top of a slope is still known as 'Wynne Cottage' or 'The Wynde'. None of these seventeenth-century winds survive, although remains of later drums can be seen in the woods of Benthall Edge, one at the top that brought limestone down to the kilns, and another that took coal and clay across the railway line to the brickworks.

Canal winds and inclined planes

The principle of the wind, developed initially for waggonways, was then applied to canals. Canal builders faced precisely the same problem as railways – it was relatively easy to reach the Gorge but hard to get down to the riverside. Two of the most ingenious solutions to this difficulty are the Hay Inclined Plane at Coalport (80) and the Brierly Hill Shafts system.

Bedlam Furnaces and the other ironworks of the 1750s and 1760s needed more raw materials than local mines could provide. There was plenty of coal and ironstone in the northern part of the coalfield but transport was expensive, so a group of businessmen came together to build a canal, linking the coal mines with the river Severn. The problem was how to get goods from the top of Blists Hill down to the riverside below. The height difference was 63m (207ft) which by conventional methods would necessitate 27 locks to get a boat from the bottom to the top. In 1788 the proprietors of the Shropshire Canal held a competition to establish, 'the best means of raising and lowering heavy weights from one navigation to another'.

There was already an inclined plane working on a canal at Ketley to the north, but the competition suggests that this might not have been an unqualified success. The contest for a new arrangement was won by Henry Williams and John Lowdon, who submitted what was basically a modification of the Ketley scheme. Boats were floated on to a cradle, which was drawn over a hump, before being wound down the railway lines. As well as using less water than traditional locks, there was a saving in

time – four men could pass a pair of boats in only three and a half minutes, a fraction of the time taken by conventional locks. The whole scheme was in operation by 1793, by which time an engine had been added to the inclined plane to provide extra power.

The Hay Inclined Plane was relatively straightforward in comparison to the complicated system at Brierly Hill, on the western branch of the canal just above Coalbrookdale (81, 82). Three different schemes were tried in ten years, before the whole lot was abandoned and replaced with a plateway on a different route.

The first scheme, operating by 1792, consisted of a pair of shafts 37m (120ft) deep. The canal divided into four arms, with the two shafts between them and a winding drum in the middle fork. A pair of cranes lifted goods out of the canal boats, and dropped them down the shafts to a plateway waggon at the bottom. The waggon emerged from a tunnel in the hillside and on to the plateway system down the Dale, with an inclined plane at the end. The planned canal at the bottom was never built but the line of the plateway can still be seen, marked by stone walls and field boundaries.

More goods were going up the shafts than coming down and there was confusion in the tunnel at the bottom. The shafts were abandoned, and an inclined plane built to the east, linked to the plateway system. This new arrangement was effective, but complicated, and when in 1800 a plateway was laid alongside the canal, a faster method was required. The old canal basin was dug away and a second incline built to get goods straight down to Coalbrookdale. Brierly Hill demonstrates the extreme difficulty of getting goods down the hill – it had taken three attempts and several modifications on the way to solve the problem. The Hay Inclined Plane was far more successful, remaining in operation until 1894.

Riverside wharfs and the promotion of Coalport

At the end of the plateway below Brierly Hill, in what is now a museum car-park, was Loadcroft Wharf. Operated by the Coalbrookdale Company it had long served as a focus for many activities: limestone was brought across the river, or down from Lincoln Hill; finished goods were exported by river; other goods were brought in from Bristol. The goods were

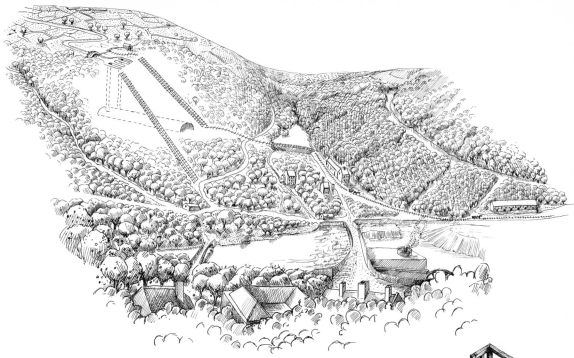

81 *Reconstruction of the Brierly Hill shaft system above Coalbrookdale. The Old Furnace can be seen in the foreground. At the top of the hill, the canal branched into four arms. Between the arms were two shafts leading to a tunnel. The system was replaced first by the inclined plane to the rear, and later by a second inclined plane* (Shelley White/Judith Dobie).

brought on a fleet of boats known as trows, which plied the Upper Severn (**83** and see **62**). The men who hauled these boats upriver were generally regarded as uncouth, with a reputation for thieving and coarse living.

Below the Hay Inclined Plane, the ironmaster William Reynolds had created a new terminus – Coalport. On a stretch of riverbank described by Thomas Telford only a few years earlier as a 'rugged uncultivated bank which scarcely produced even grass', a busy port had grown up, with loading facilities, warehouses, industries and houses.

The promotion of Coalport was every bit as deliberate as Darby's promotion of the Iron Bridge. In 1788 Richard Reynolds bought the land there from Abraham Darby III, and leased it to his son William who encouraged new industries to locate there; as well as the Coalport China Works which still stand, there was

82 *Winding arrangement at Brierly Hill. The winding drum and pulley system were located on top of the four canal arms* (see **81**) (Greg Day/Hickton Madeley Design).

a timber yard, a bag factory, a ropeworks and plans for a chemical factory. Thirty houses were built for workmen and the most spectacular feature was a huge stone warehouse, spanning the area between the canal and the riverside, built in 1792 (**colour plate 8**). The footings can still be seen today, alongside the big stone blocks of Reynolds' wharfs.

83 *The Iron Bridge, 1784, T.F. Burney. Four men may be seen bow-hauling a trow upstream, while on the other side of the river, goods are unloaded. There is a stagecoach on the bridge and packhorses on a road* (SSMT 33).

Today there is little trace of activity at Coalport but it was once very busy; its boats left for Bristol every Spring Tide and there were daily boats to Bridgnorth, Bewdley, Gloucester and Stourport. True to its name, coal became one of the major exports, and goods for the towns of Newport, Shifnal and Wellington were all brought into the area via the Coalport wharfs.

Coalport was successful because it provided a much needed link between the river Severn, the industries of the Gorge, and the towns and industrial areas in the land-locked northern part of the coalfield. By 1835 it also provided a link through to the national canal network,

with the construction of a new junction at Wappenshall to the north. But for all its advantages, Coalport depended upon the river Severn remaining a usable transport link.

The river Severn and life on the riverside

Transport on the river Severn had never been easy; because the river could only be used reliably during winter months, firms could only market their goods for half of the year. Added to that, boats often went aground on the old fords and fish weirs. Early in 1800 Thomas Telford remarked that navigation was getting more difficult with the drainage of water meadows and things did not improve over the ensuing years. Nevertheless, industry remained dependent upon the river until the 1860s.

Old illustrations suggest that most riverside wharfs were far more casual affairs than either Coalport or Loadcroft Wharf, with boats tied up alongside a stretch of river bank and goods carried ashore across a plank. Occasionally stone walls suggest former wharfs, such as

84 *The Coalport Ferry, c.1900–10* (IGMT 1981.3369).

those at Coalford, or the collapsed walls in the river at Calcutts, but in general archaeology shows that built wharf arrangements were rare.

Despite this lack of formal building, access to the riverbank was a valuable asset and strictly controlled. James Clifford had owned 'wharf places' opposite each of his coal mines in 1608, while John Weld in 1630 had agonized over how he was to get access down the riverside. Two hundred years later the Tithe Map of 1840 shows how each brick- and tile-maker had a special loading place for his own goods on the riverside, linked through to the brickworks. Access to the river was very necessary to any industrial operation, even after the construction of the canal system.

The riverside also became a focus of settlement. From the early 1700s, small communities grew up along the riverbank, often concentrated around individual industries. The best example is at Jackfield, where a string of little clusters developed – Yates Coppice, Ladywood, Barnetts Leasow, Hollygreaves, The Calcutts, Jackfield, Salthouses, The Tuckies, The Werps, Severn Cottages, the Woodbridge and Gitchfield. The names come from local landmarks, old houses, field names or riverside industrial activities. Archaeological evidence shows that the Salthouses and Jackfield were areas of pottery manufacture, while the census of 1841 shows that watermen congregated at Hollygreaves. Most of these communities have now gone, lost through a combination of dereliction, the construction of the railway and spectacular land slips, but a few of the little brick cottages in Jackfield today reflect the appearance of these communities: groups of small cottages with a shop or two, but never the urban development of Ironbridge.

Amongst these small cottages was the occasional fine house – the timber-framed Dog and Duck, now demolished, or Calcutts House, still standing in Jackfield, built in 1755. Similar large dwellings can be found in Ironbridge, at Dale End, or formerly standing at the end of the Free Bridge. These buildings originated as the homes of entrepreneurs, often barge-owners or coal miners. Their houses were sited away from the traditional farm lands, next to mines or the riverbank, reflecting the activities of the owners.

Crossing the river

River ferries also influenced the growth of settlement (84). One of the earliest was known as Adams Ferry, at the site of the present Free Bridge. The cluster of settlement at Madeley Wood and the large seventeenth-century timber-framed buildings on either side, suggest that this had long been an important river crossing. From the 1790s there was also a ferry at The Werps which carried workers from their homes in Jackfield to the Coalport China works; in 1799 the ferry sank, drowning 29 people.

Owning or controlling a ferry was a valuable asset, and the construction of the Iron Bridge on the site of a ferry crossing clearly posed a threat to the owners of others. There was some compensation – in exchange for giving up his ferry, the landowner could claim free passage across the bridge – but at the same time, the bridge trustees added a clause restricting any ferry from operating within a certain distance of the new bridge.

This link between ferry sites and later bridges can be seen elsewhere in the Gorge. Adams Ferry, for example, was replaced by the first toll-free crossing of the river Severn, the Haynes Memorial (or Free Bridge), built in 1909. This is the main bridge by which cars cross the river today, and was funded by local subscription. The Hennebique-Mouchel technique of concrete construction was chosen because it was cheap and the bridge could be constructed without coffer dams. The second toll-free crossing, the Coalport and Jackfield Memorial footbridge of 1922 (85), replaced the fateful Coalport ferry, and was built in memory of those who died in the First World War.

The Iron Bridge was not the only bridge to

be built across the river in 1779. At Coalport to the east, a bridge using traditional wooden construction was built. It was damaged in the floods of 1795 and rebuilt using iron ribs with a timber superstructure. Confidence in cast iron was such that by 1817, when one rib fractured, it was decided to rebuild the whole bridge in iron, using the original ribs. The iron was supplied by local ironmasters, Onions and Banks; the bridge remains today the earliest cast-iron bridge still used by vehicles (86).

It is often claimed that Thomas Telford was involved in the construction of the Iron Bridge. He was not, but as County Surveyor for Shropshire he was involved in the repairs to many bridges after the floods of 1795, and also in the construction of a new bridge to replace the damaged medieval bridge at Buildwas. The Buildwas Bridge (see 67) was in a sense an experiment, and it later became clear that Telford had underestimated the huge pressure on either end of the abutments. When the bridge he built was eventually replaced in 1905–6 by a steel Pratt Truss, the engineers placed the ends of the new bridge on rollers, which allowed for continuing movement of the banks of the river. The bridge since then twice reached its limit, and had to be lifted and refixed, before being replaced in 1992.

The bridges over the river Severn changed the whole geography of the Gorge – the old hillside tracks were replaced by new roads such as the Broseley Road and Madeley Hill, often involving extraordinary feats of engineering. The old separation between the communities of the north and south, with their focus on Broseley or Madeley, was replaced by a new, inward looking geography with the growth of Ironbridge as an urban centre in the Gorge itself.

The standard-gauge railway network

Although the river had provided a comparative advantage in the seventeenth century, by the

85 (Above, right) *The opening of the Coalport and Jackfield Memorial Bridge in 1922* (IGMT 1984.6424).

86 (Below, right) *Coalport Bridge, photographed 1900–5* (IGMT 1980.1790).

Opening of Colport and Jackfield Memorial Bridge.

beginning of the nineteenth century the Gorge was becoming isolated as first canals, and later railways, made other manufacturing areas more competitive.

Many people hoped that the solution lay in the railway network which reached the Gorge with the construction of the London and North Western Railway line to Blists Hill and Coalport in 1860, the Severn Valley Railway section of the Great Western Railway in 1862 and the Coalbrookdale branch of the Great Western Railway in 1864. Three lines linked the Gorge to the rest of the country. There was a station at Coalport, another which survives as a private house on the southern side of the Coalport Bridge, and a station known as Ironbridge and Broseley, on the south side of the Iron Bridge (87). There were halts at Coalbrookdale and Jackfield, and a fine level crossing gate still

stands at Jackfield. Building the railway line involved demolishing a good number of houses at Jackfield, creating dramatic viaducts which hug the steep south bank of the river with cuttings through the pools and ironworks of Coalbrookdale. The tension between the old transport systems and the new is visible in the elaborate bridges to keep the old plateway networks at Blists Hill and Benthall Edge in operation, and in agreements which prevented competition with the Hay Inclined Plane.

The new lines did bring benefits – the Craven Dunnill and Maws works were built alongside the railway lines, and the new phases of building at Coalbrookdale in 1880 suggest an increasing demand for products. New railway sidings were built at Blists Hill and on Benthall Edge and the old riverside wharfs began to fall into disuse. Goods could now be transported at any time of the year. The railway was a key factor in the siting of the power station opened in 1932 and in full commission by 1939, the last major new industry to come to the area.

The Ironbridge Gorge – like elsewhere – fell prey to the railway closures of the 1960s. In

87 *View of Ironbridge and Broseley station, c.1900–5, with a steam locomotive in the middle distance. The station is now the site of a visitors' car-park* (IGMT 1982.1873).

1967 the last passenger train travelled over the Coalbrookdale viaduct, down the valley, across the river on the splendid Albert Edward Bridge (designed by John Fowler) and up towards Much Wenlock and Shrewsbury. The line remains in use for coal, but now stops at the power station. The Severn Valley Railway closed in 1970, but the line, viaduct and bridges remain. From Bridgnorth to Kidderminster it now operates as a successful, volunteer-run railway. The Coalport line closed to passengers in 1952 and to freight in 1960, and remains as a footpath.

The railway failed to have a lasting impact, however; the ironworks had closed long ago, and the prestigious products of the 1880s began to lose out to fashion and war-time austerity. Despite the construction of the railway, the Gorge had never become a centre of population or demand. Markets were always elsewhere, and as the coal and other minerals ran out, raw materials too were dependent upon transport. Instead the late nineteenth century and early twentieth century saw the growth of other industrial areas elsewhere, at the expense of Ironbridge.

9

Victorian Ironbridge

In the first few decades of the nineteenth century, the iron industry was winding down. Trade was at a low ebb, and there was a degree of pessimism about the prospects for manufacturing. Yet by mid-century, the town of Ironbridge had become a highly respectable place to live. The Coalport China manufactory was flourishing and the Coalbrookdale Company was producing a new range of artistic products. The Gorge had moved away from heavy industry, towards the deliberate promotion of fine goods to a discerning market; there was a new emphasis on craftsmanship and skill, elegance and refinement. This move was reflected in the buildings of the period – churches, chapels, schools and institutes, and even industrial structures which were more decorative than their predecessors.

While the sunny slopes of Ironbridge became a most desirable place to build a villa, Jackfield in the midst of the brick and tile works was described by H.P Dunnill as,

> not all the world, but a very poor bit of the fag end of it...made up of old pit shafts, pit mounds, rubbish heaps, brick ends, broken drain and roof and paving tiles, dilapidated houses, sloughy lanes and miry roads.

The skilled employees of the Coalbrookdale Company built themselves new houses, whereas the brick and tile workers had no security, and worked long hours for little pay. Yet it was in the midst of this squalor that two huge new factories were built to make encaustic tiles – patterned wall and floor tiles, suitable for churches and public buildings.

This contrast between the mundane and the ornate, between decay and elegance was a theme which persisted throughout the nine-teenth century. Despite the fine china, art castings and decorative tiles, most of the local industrial output consisted of ordinary goods such as kitchen pottery, domestic iron goods, drainpipes, bricks and roof tiles.

Art castings

Most of the blast furnaces in the Gorge shut down as operations moved north to be closer to supplies of raw materials. Following a change of management in 1830 the Coalbrook-dale Company reorganized, moving smelting to Lightmoor, and concentrating on casting at Coalbrookdale. They would produce anything from a 'tenpenny three-legged pot, or an humble matter-of-fact frying pan, to a powerful motor, a superbly artistic gateway or a metallic Venus de Medici'. Through their display at the Great Exhibition of 1851 they became internationally famous for fine castings, and the gates they exhibited remain today near the Albert Hall serving as a permanent advertisement for the company's products in the same way as the Iron Bridge had done nearly a hundred years earlier. In the catalogue for the exhibition, they claimed to be the biggest ironworks in the world, with an output of 2000 tons a week and a workforce of 3–4000 people.

With the new emphasis on fine products came a requirement to provide a respectable front to the ramshackle group of ironworking sheds that comprised the Coalbrookdale works. The present Museum of Iron, for example, was built in 1838 as a grand new warehouse, dominating the valley; an ornamental clock was added later, in 1843, as a prominent example of Coalbrookdale cast iron. At the bottom of the valley, facing out over the river Severn is the Severn Warehouse (89), built at about the same time

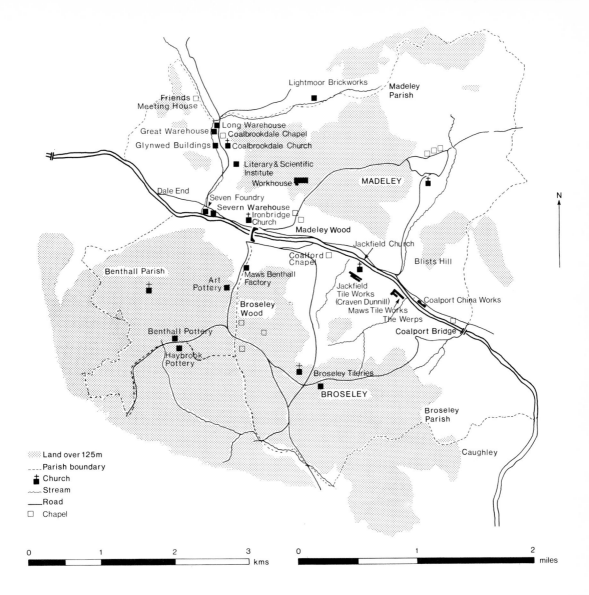

88 Victorian sites and buildings mentioned in the text (Judith Dobie).

by an anonymous architect (perhaps Samuel Cookson) who added castellated turrets, mock arrow loops and pointed windows to an ordinary riverside warehouse. A new art department and modelling room were added to the main ironworking complex at the top of the valley, with light, airy rooms and fine new offices. Many of the artists who worked there would have been trained at the School of Art, founded in 1856 and housed in the new Literary and Scientific Institute built by the company as an adult education centre for its employees in 1859 (**90**).

The changing image of the firm can also be seen in the lifestyle of the Darby family members who began both to play a greater role in local politics and to be more prominent in society than earlier generations had been. Alfred Darby, son of Abraham Darby IV rebelled against the restrained Quakerism of his family by becoming an Anglican. He endowed the Coalbrookdale Church, commissioning the design from a firm of London architects, and bought Stanley Hall near Bridgnorth, thus

89 *The ornate Severn Warehouse, built c.1840.*

suggesting that he was keen to be as much a landowner and patron of the arts as an ironworks manager.

Art castings had only ever represented a small proportion of the company's output (**91**), while the bulk of it consisted of engineering products and domestic goods (**92**). Many of the buildings which still stand were intended to house this type of production – the big engineering shop was built in the 1880s for assembling engines, the Severn Foundry at the bottom of the Dale was built in 1901 to accommodate the demand for gas cookers and fireplaces created by the boom in London council housing. One of the main difficulties in the archaeology of industrial buildings is establishing the original function from the building alone, as often they are little more than sheds. Few records survive, and most buildings were probably designed by

the works manager to a general model. The original purpose of the other surviving Coalbrookdale Company buildings, such as the one with the saw-tooth roof or the Long Warehouse in the 1880s, for example, are now lost. Fortunately, early descriptions of the workings of the other great nineteenth-century group of industrial buildings, the encaustic tileworks, do survive.

The encaustic tile industry
Today it is possible for the visitor to enter the Jackfield Tile Museum housed in the old encaustic tileworks (**colour plate 15**) and walk up the stairs to the gaslit showroom over the arch to view the range of tiles produced by the firm, set in panels on the walls, very much as a nineteenth-century customer might have done (**colour plate 14**). The earlier customer would most likely have been an architect or builder, choosing decorative tiles to adorn the walls or floor of a church or public building,

90 *The Literary and Scientific Institute built in 1859 by the Coalbrookdale Company to provide education for its employees* (IGMT).

perhaps as far afield as Brazil or Australia. He might have been offered a panel of wall tiles with a decorative moulded dado rail, or a simple, geometric tile pavement, perhaps with a decorative border, possibly suitable for a hallway. Had he been one of the many architects involved in the renovation of churches in the second half of the nineteenth century, he might have chosen reproductions of medieval floor tiles using the same techniques as the originals. More expensive products included one-off, hand painted panels depicting nursery characters for a children's hospital, or rural scenes for a dairy.

A favoured customer might also have been offered a tour of the works. The showrooms and offices at the front were just a small part of the complex, which had been designed expressly to accommodate the many different processes of tile-making from clay preparation right through to sales and packing.

The factory had been designed by Charles Lynam, a Stoke-on-Trent architect who specialized in public buildings, but who had become involved in the design of tile factories through his contacts with the firm of Mintons. The links with Stoke and the pottery industry can be seen in the front of the building, which resembles the entrance to a pot bank – an arched entrance facing the street with offices, with manufacturing buildings grouped to the rear. Lynam has used many of the motifs which characterize his

Improved House Pump, brass clack,
reversible cap and handle, with
bored iron working barrel.
12 in. tail piece for cast pipe.

92 *House waterpump from Coalbrookdale
Company's 1875 catalogue (IGMT 1989.4309).*

91 *Coalbrookdale cast-iron fountain, c.1880*
(IGMT 1986.14013).

other work – pointed window heads filled with
examples of encaustic tiles, decorative brick
and the tower, now missing its roof.

The architect had had to contend with a very
difficult site which in 1874 housed a rundown
and dilapidated pottery. Archaeological evidence shows that tiles had successfully been
made in one of the old kilns, but when H.P.
Dunnill took over the site he decided that in
order to accommodate the efficient production
of tiles, purpose-built works were required (**93**).
The old pottery remained standing, while a new
one was laid out, squeezed between the pottery
and the recently completed railway line.

The buildings that can be seen today differ
in some ways from the original layout. Soon
after the buildings were finished, alterations
began – new down-draught kilns were built to

the east, later to be replaced by a tunnel kiln.
Tile-making continued until the middle of this
century when the factory was taken over by a
brass founder and manufacturer of brick and
tile machines. In 1952 a firm of precision engineers, Marshall Osborne, took over, finally
closing in 1982. Although most of the old
tile-making equipment was removed, and the
buildings altered it is still possible to trace the
movement of clay from the mine to the mills,
the storage bins, the pressing and decorating
areas. The bases of the down-draught kilns can
still be seen, and of course the offices and
showroom survive as a reminder of the last
stage of the process.

The Craven Dunnill tileworks was the fourth
encaustic tileworks here, and soon after it
opened another was built to the east. The
demand for tiles in the Victorian period began
in response to the programme of church restoration in the 1850s, and was promoted by architects such as Augustus Pugin who made great
use of reproduction tiles in paving (**colour
plate 13**). William Exley had in fact been
making encaustic tiles at his Jackfield brick-

93 *Engraving of the Craven Dunnill encaustic tileworks, opened in 1874.*

works since 1835. Exley must have been successful, as Mintons of Stoke went to the trouble of threatening legal action for infringement of their patent.

George and Arthur Maw set up an encaustic tile manufactory in 1852 at Benthall. It was on the site of the old ironworks to make use of the clay which was the principal attraction of the Gorge for the Maws. The local supplies of red clays had long been used for the manufacture of soft red floor tiles, and the white clays mined near Bedlam had been exported down the river to Worcester, where the Maws had used them in their tile factory there. George Maw (**94**) was an accomplished geologist, who had made a detailed study of all the clays of Britain and decided that the clays of Benthall best suited his needs. Coal for firing kilns was also readily available in the neighbourhood, and the river Severn provided transport.

The Benthall factory became cramped as buildings spilled across the road on to the other side of the narrow valley, and piles of broken tiles began to fill the area. In spite of these unpropitious surroundings, Maws filed many new patents during the 1860s and 1870s. They invented a new way of making tiles using dry clay dust, which reduced the amount of shrinkage; they began to make mosaics; experimented with different glazes and finishes; and introduced steam power for the first time in 1873. These new methods of production must have been difficult to fit into the old works, and the company searched for a new site.

The new Maws factory which opened in 1883 was once the largest encaustic tile manufactory in the world, and still stands today. It was designed by Charles Lynam, on entirely new principles, to incorporate steam-driven machinery. The entrance and offices survive, some of the workshops have been converted into small industrial units, and the clay mill and storage bins have just been transformed into houses. But the old kilns, brickworks, tunnel kiln,

gasworks and other buildings have now been demolished. Because the site was so big, production could be more flexible than at other sites, and it remained in operation until 1969.

Maws and Craven Dunnill tiles, and those from the Broseley Tileries, a roof-tile manufactory to the north, achieved an international reputation in the later part of the nineteenth century. Their tile floors adorned public buildings such as Manchester Town Hall, notable pubs such as the Crown Bar in Belfast, and a range of buildings overseas, for example cathedrals in Sydney and Melbourne. Like the Coalbrookdale works, they employed artists to design their products and were anxious to promote an image of design excellence and quality (**colour plate 12**).

The production of art pottery (see Chapter 5) was another example of the general concern with art and design at the end of the nineteenth century (**colour plate 11**). Encaustic tiles (**colour plate 14**), art pottery, terracotta and art castings were all prestigious products, heavily promoted at a national and international level through exhibitions and coloured catalogues (**95**). The aim would have been to produce a high-value product which would compensate for the difficulties and high transport costs of the Gorge. There was never a great concentration of population and in order to survive manufacturers had to reach a wider market with a specialist product.

Yet there was something more than a concern for high profits. The new products involved conscious design to a much greater degree than anything produced previously in the Gorge, and were part of a quest for respectability which can be seen in many different ways. At the top level, it was a matter of country seats and the patronage of the arts, while for some of the workforce at least, it involved education, skills and a better standard of living. Some of this can be seen in the growth of the town of Ironbridge.

The town of Ironbridge

The biggest transformation in the Victorian period was the growth of the town of Ironbridge

94 *Portrait of George Maw with three children, 1873* (IGMT 1983.1329).

itself. The name Ironbridge first appeared as a postal address in 1805, gradually supplanting Coalbrookdale or Madeley Wood, until it became the general name for the area. Before the construction of the bridge, there was no town as it exists today.

Madeley Wood, the largest community, lay to the east (**96**). It had a population of over 3500 people at the end of the eighteenth century, living in houses clustered at the top of the hill, and scattered down the hillside towards the old ferry. It was an industrialized community, and included public houses and a Methodist meeting house, but little in the way of formal shops. There was another small community to the west of modern Ironbridge at Dale End where houses and small industries focused on the Loadcroft Wharf. Here was a row of nailmakers' houses, a soap house and a timber yard. Along what is today the Wharfage there were several cottages, including at least one fine brick house, most likely belonging to a relatively wealthy barge-owner.

This pattern of small settlements was typical of the Gorge. There were clusters of houses spread about the valley along the riverside at Jackfield, and on the slopes above the Gorge. Many of these communities were orientated towards individual industries; for example, the china workers at Coalport lived at The Werps on the south bank, ironworkers were concentrated at Coalbrookdale and trow men at Bower Yard. These settlements had no real focus, and relatively little in the way of tradesmen. The commercial centres for the area remained the town of Madeley on the north bank, Broseley on the south bank and to some extent Much Wenlock, the administrative centre of the area. It was here that markets were held and trades congregated.

The growth of Ironbridge in the nineteenth century created the first commercial, almost urban, centre within the Gorge itself. The nucleus of the town emerged soon after the construction of the Iron Bridge, with the building of the Tontine Hotel, the new market place and the laying out of new roads (see Chapter 7). By the 1790s there were shops around the edge of the bridge and along the Wharfage, some of which were quite substantial. In the first few decades of the nineteenth century, the town was transformed into a busy, thriving centre. By 1837, Ironbridge was, according to Charles Hulbert,

the merchantile part of the town of Madeley... the focus of professional and commercial pursuits. The weekly market, the Post Office, the Printing Office, principal inns, Drapery, Grocery and Ironmongery, Watch Making, Cabinet Making, Timber and Boat Building establishments; Subscription Library, Subscription Dispensary, Branch Bank, Subscription Baths, Gentlemen of the Legal and medical professions, Ladies Boarding School, etc

In the 1830s the town was much busier than it is today. There were new, purpose-built shops in the centre of town; for instance, what is now the 'Shop in the Square' was built by 1829. The spaces along the Wharfage were filled in to create an almost continuous line of shops. Many of the earlier buildings such as the Savings Bank of 1828 and the shops and buildings on both sides of the north end of the bridge have now been demolished. Where the roundabout is today there was another continuous row of shops and buildings, creating a much larger and more built-up town.

New brick villas were built above the town, set in garden plots along the hillside. These houses had fine views over the wooded south bank of the river (avoiding the smoke of Jackfield), and faced south to catch the sun; they suggest that Ironbridge had become a fashionable place to live. One of the most striking is Orchard House, built c.1843 by the brickmaker William Davis, clearly to show off the range of local brick products. The house has a patterned tile roof, decorative chimneys and terracotta detailing.

Between these houses were the smaller, earlier brick cottages, some of which were replaced by new houses or rebuilt as land values rose. From the 1850s onwards, more and more smaller houses were built, but with some degree of pretension, with symmetrical facades and architectural details, which were much finer than the earlier workers' cottages.

95 *Coalbrookdale Company statues at the Kensington Olympia Exhibition, 1889* (IGMT 1983.316).

96 *Houses on the riverside at Madeley Wood c.1890, including the timber-framed Lloyds* (IGMT 1988.284)

Despite this level of respectability Ironbridge remained a fairly rough area with a poor reputation for behaviour. It also had a large number of public houses. Along the Wharfage today are the White Hart, the Malthouse and the Swan (**97**), all of which were originally licensed in the late eighteenth century. Although the new bridge would have assisted trade, these must still have catered largely for the local industrial workers and barge-men. Beer would originally have been brewed at home in the traditional 'brewhouse', but gradually malting and brewing became the preserve of the professional publican. The large building to the left of the Malthouse originally housed the floors where the barley germinated, and the kiln where the barley was roasted remains today in a building to the rear.

Churches and chapels

The contrast between the poorer working men and the better off groups in society can be seen in the battle for souls – the tension between church and chapel. The buildings that survive and their positions give us some idea of the religious geography and aspirations of the people who lived in the area.

The fact that Ironbridge was chosen as the site for a new church in 1837 confirms that by then Ironbridge was established as a local centre. The church was built by the Church Commissioners, as part of a programme to provide low cost churches in areas where it was felt that there was no proper accommodation for the new industrial classes. Until then, the only church in the Gorge had been the Red Church on the hill above Jackfield; otherwise the nearest churches were in Broseley and Madeley.

The lack of church provision was also an indication of the strength of non-conformism. John Fletcher, the vicar of Madeley from 1760 onwards, was a charismatic preacher, who adopted the teachings of John Wesley, and built up a strong following. At the same time as the new church was being built in Ironbridge, a new Wesleyan Methodist chapel was constructed in Madeley Wood, the older community to the east which had a long tradition of non-conformism. The church and the chapel are quite similar in their use of galleries that are supported on iron pillars and simple, unornamented brick construction. The chapel was designed by Samuel Smith of Madeley, and is

97 *The Swan public house* (IGMTAU)

of brick with cast-iron windows, replacing an earlier chapel of 1776 which still stands. There were other chapels in the older industrial settlements – on the opposite bank of the river at Jackfield was a small Wesleyan Chapel built in 1825. Again it is a very plain building, of brick with tall narrow windows and cast-iron window frames. In Coalbrookdale, an earlier chapel of 1785 was replaced in 1885 by a large and ornate red-brick building, which dominates the valley today (**98**).

This trend towards a greater degree of architectural pretension is visible in the later churches. Soon after the Ironbridge church was completed, the Coalbrookdale church was built in 1854, to the design of Reeves and Voysey of London. In 1863, the Church of St Mary in Jackfield was consecrated, designed by the architect A.W. Blomfield in polychromatic brick, with terracotta and stone dressings (**colour plate 9**). Both churches are much more ornate than the Ironbridge church and, through

the employment of noted architects, reflect a much greater concern for appearance and opinion.

For all its pretensions, Ironbridge never became a large town with a central role in local administration. It was certainly prosperous – the range of trades and shops in Ironbridge was greater than that of neighbouring towns, and its growing status could be seen in the provision of public buildings – a police station in 1862, and the Madeley Union Workhouse on the top of the hill in 1874, as well as a dispensary, several new schools and two gas companies. Some civic functions did move to Ironbridge from Much Wenlock; but there was never a formal town. Sanitation remained primitive and in the 1860s, when water from the river was still being sold by the bucketfull, the area was ravaged by fever. New industries, and even

98 *Coalbrookdale Chapel, built overlooking the works in 1885* (Michael Worthington).

99 *The Crown Inn, Hodge Bower, whose landlord was one of the first to promote tourism in the area* (Michael Worthington).

the construction of the railways, had failed to bring lasting prosperity, and many people began to move out of the area.

By the end of the century, Ironbridge was described as, 'tiers of dirty cottages'; slag and spoil heaps disfigured the riverside, and there was a sense that the 'best days were past'. The earliest photographs show the dereliction and decay, particularly along the south side of the river. Yet it seems that the old contrasts persisted, and that Ironbridge itself retained an element of respectability.

Tourists were beginning to visit the area in small numbers. The owner of the Crown Inn on Hodge Bower, above Ironbridge, was promoting the idea of a day out in the Gorge, with lunch included (**99**). Postcards of the Iron Bridge and other prominent sights were published by a local firm. Visitors from school boys to industrialists were starting to recognize the significance of the area and its monuments, and there were the first glimmers of a revival of interest which was to culminate in the restoration of the Gorge as it is today.

10

The admiration of strangers

Today hundreds of thousands of visitors come to the Gorge each year, some to the complex of museums and many just to see the Iron Bridge. Tourism, however, is by no means a new industry; the eighteenth century was a period of enquiry – those who could afford it travelled abroad, those who could not observed the wonders of Britain.

A most noble scenery

Even before the construction of the bridge, travellers would visit Coalbrookdale to gaze upon the fine view from the hills above the valley and the pillars of flame and smoke at the bottom. Once the bridge was built, it became the centrepiece, attracting huge numbers of visitors. Some were interested in the technicalities of cast iron, but for most the fascination lay in the contrast between the romantic and the frightening, the pleasant wooded hillsides and 'all the horrors that art might conceive' at the bottom. The Gorge was likened to a scene from Dante, the, 'epitome of infernal regions' (**colour plate 4**), and the bridge, set between two dramatic hills resembled 'that fatal bridge made by sin and death over chaos, from the boundaries of hell to the wall of this now defenceless world'.

Some of those who came to see the bridge were spies. Britain's technical successes were a source of envy, and foreign countries sent envoys to investigate the developments of their competitors. Marchant de la Houlière who visited the area in 1775 was a French government spy, Joseph Ritter von Baader who sketched the first iron rails was Bavarian, and a Venetian, several Poles, Americans, Swedes and Germans all left with very detailed accounts of what they had observed. In

response to this, many of the local ironmasters became very secretive about their works, and would deny access to visitors.

Not everybody who wrote about or drew the bridge had been to Ironbridge. Pictures were copied over and over again, and can be recognized by the same coach which constantly crosses the bridge, or the same mistakes, such as including the extra rib before it had been built. Descriptions too were plagiarized – a technical passage by Phillips was used in an edition of Camden's *Britannia*, which was subsequently quoted by almost all the nineteenth-century tourist guides.

A gloomy and murky district

As the ironworks closed and the area became derelict, the visitors stopped coming. Into the diaries and letters of those people who did, crept a critical note – the furnaces were run down, the Iron Bridge a poor design, the conditions of the workmen appalling and the area gloomy (**100**). Yet it is possible to trace amidst this pessimism a change in the perception of the Gorge from a technical wonder to a place of historical significance. Fifty years after it was built, the bridge was beginning to be recognized as an historical achievement in its own right. It was not until fifty years after that that the first trickle of visitors interested in the past began to arrive. The Coalbrookdale Company and others were, by this time, happy to welcome visitors and actively promoted their links with the past. Perhaps they saw this as an opportunity to lend their firms a degree of respectability, rooted in generation after generation of achievement.

Realistically, a visitor would have been confronted with a derelict landscape. Mining scars,

100 *A row of houses in Ironbridge, c.1900. Few houses were built in this period, and most of the existing housing stock became very run down* (IGMT 1982.1863).

bare hills, empty buildings, broken-down houses and open sewers. Industries were closing and had left vast heaps of waste of all types – broken tiles, boiler ash, slag, casting sand. The slag at least was crushed and recycled for road mending, but the rest remained. There were some signs of life – during the Second World War the government had encouraged firms to move into some of the old buildings to escape the London bombs, so that the china works which had closed in 1926, for example, was used for making rubber mats, lipsticks and car exhausts. Nevertheless, housing was declared insanitary, roads were bad and almost a third of the old coalfield area was affected by instability from the abandoned mines below the surface.

Telford New Town

The outlook seemed poor until 1963 when the coalfield, including the Ironbridge Gorge, was designated a New Town. The aim was to encour-

age industry and housing to move out of Birmingham and the Black Country, into a brand new, planned environment. Pit heaps were cleared, mine shafts capped and a new network of roads and estates was laid out.

At first the Ironbridge Gorge was set aside with the intention of recreating the beauty that the Gorge had lost over the past 400 years. There was a programme of tree planting and even the demolition of unsightly old buildings. Within a few years, there was a subtle change in the official attitude: industrial remains were beginning to be accepted as worth preserving. It was soon recognized that the whole area was full of remains and the Gorge was declared first a Conservation Area in 1967, and then in 1986 a World Heritage Site.

Industrial archaeology

One of the reasons behind this change of heart was the growing interest in industrial archaeology. The Newcomen Society was founded in 1919 to bring together people interested in the history of engineering. The emphasis was on technology rather than archaeology, and most of those involved were able to apply professional skills in engineering, geology or industry to the study of the past.

101 *Cover building erected over the Darby Furnace. Although controversial in design, the building has been effective in protecting the old masonry from weather damage* (Michael Worthington).

The concern of the engineering profession in fact saved the Iron Bridge. In 1902 a report had recommended repairs to the Bridge, and a few years later the Free Bridge was built to relieve it of traffic. A second report in 1923 expressed deep concern about the continuing traffic, and concluded that, given the historical value of the bridge, the best option was to restrict the loading. The promoters of the new power station objected, and put forward a plan to demolish the bridge and build a new concrete one. The Newcomen Society visited the bridge in 1924 and expressed great concern about their proposal. Perhaps partly as a result of pressure from them, nothing came of the plan, and in 1934 it was scheduled as an Ancient Monument. The power station built a new bridge to the west.

Since then interest in industrial archaeology has continued to grow, fuelled by amateur groups and Worker's Education Classes in the 1950s, and more recently by some of the great battles over such icons as the Euston Arch, demolished in 1962. Traditional archaeologists, too, have become increasingly involved in industrial sites, although there is an ongoing debate about the relative virtues of archaeological and engineering skills in dealing with these sites.

The Ironbridge Gorge Museums

The museums in the Ironbridge Gorge were a product of this increasing concern for the preservation of industrial sites, together with the opportunities created by the establishment of a new town. Abraham Darby's furnace had had been excavated in 1959 (**101**), and the site already housed a small museum set up by Allied Ironfounders. In 1967 the Ironbridge Gorge Museum Trust was set up with a much broader remit to care for objects of industrial and historical interest over the whole area. The problem was that there were too many sites to be covered by one museum.

Instead of trying to recreate industrial relics in a conventional museum setting with labels, an open-air museum was set up at Blists Hill, centred around the old blast furnaces and brickworks there (**102**). Objects which might otherwise have been scrapped were dismantled and moved to Blists Hill, and placed in the context of a recreated nineteenth-century village. The old furnaces were dug out, parts of the brickworks brought into use as stores, and the museum opened to the public in 1973. At the old Coalbrookdale site, the furnace was covered, the Great Warehouse turned into a Museum of Iron and the remaining Long Warehouse converted to house a library and offices. The Coalport China works became a museum, the Severn Warehouse a visitors' centre and the Jackfield tileworks a museum of tiles and centre for tile manufacturing. Rosehill, the old Darby house, was restored and the Bedlam Furnaces and Hay Inclined Plane cleared and renovated.

The museums brought tourists – some 400,000 each year – which in turn created an industry of hotels and guesthouses, shops and restaurants. Boats are seen on the river, coaches park on the site of the old railway station. The Gorge is once again a busy, crowded place, focused upon that engineering marvel, the Iron Bridge.

The history of the Gorge is not at an end, nor are all the battles to conserve it won, but the issues today are not so much about persuading a sceptical public of the importance of the area, but of coping intelligently with its very popularity. The dilapidated houses have nearly all been renovated, the bridge and its precincts tidied, flowers bloom in spaces where

102 *School children at Blists Hill. Education is a major function of the museum, with over 90,000 educational visits each year* (IGMT).

old buildings once stood, and traffic is slowed and channelled to an acceptable pace. Dealing with the number of cars can be a problem, as can getting visitors to each of the sites, and there are still threats – a recent public inquiry into a proposed new bridge across the Gorge highlighted the difficulty of balancing commerce and aesthetics.

Nevertheless, the Gorge remains a wonderful and important place where a series of extraordinary events took place. There is a huge amount of archaeological evidence remaining, perhaps preserved by the very stagnation of the nineteenth century. The pattern of the landscape, with its jumble of houses, industrial buildings, old railway lines and monuments, still provides us with the historical framework in which to see, and understand, that extraordinary monument, the Iron Bridge.

Why was the bridge built here?

There were several factors: a valley which had for some time been a commercial backwater, and whose steep sides made building a bridge

a major undertaking requiring a radical solution; a group of entrepreneurs who were able to raise the finance, and who included John Wilkinson and Abraham Darby III, both men who were utterly convinced of the feasibility of a cast-iron bridge, and who, at the same time, were keen to demonstrate their products to the world. Finally, a good design and a careful choice of site, which meant that the bridge did not suffer the fate of many other bridges on the Severn, including Telford's iron bridge at Buildwas.

Why did so much happen in this small area?

The Ironbridge Gorge had many advantages for industry – raw materials, water-power and a transport link with Bristol, but events depend upon people. The first generation of entrepreneurs opened up the Gorge through the coal industry, and adopted ingenious solutions to the problem of moving coal around the valley. By the end of the seventeenth century there was an industrial workforce, a transport network and the capital to invest in new ventures. Into this area came a close-knit group of men and women, linked by a common bond of religion and a work ethic – the Darbys, Reynolds, their works managers and their associates.

103 *Group portrait on the last day of the Coalport China Works, 1926* (IGMT 1980.1724).

They in turn built links with other innovators – John Curr who invented plateway rails, Boulton and Watt who built steam engines, Richard Trevithick, experimenting with the first locomotives.

Was there really an Industrial Revolution?

The idea of the Industrial Revolution is constantly being questioned, and for archaeologists may fall out of favour in the same way as the Neolithic (or farming) revolution has. In any industry it is possible to find examples which contradict the idea of a massive increase in production in the late eighteenth century – pipemaking for example, in which machinery was only introduced in the late nineteenth century; coal-mining where the increase in output was in the seventeenth century; tilemaking where the output grew immeasurably in the 1870s and 1880s. Equally, there were transformations in industries not normally associated with the Industrial Revolution – the new brick and tile manufactories on the riverside in the late eighteenth century, the mass production of coarse domestic pottery at a similar date.

However, one major change did take place here and altered the whole face of manufacturing. In 1754 there were two old blast furnaces, within five years nine more had been built. All produced iron with coke which could be turned into wrought iron, all were using engines to recycle water, all were run by large companies which integrated different aspects of their operation, such as transport and coal-mining and all were on greenfield sites. By any standards this represents an unprecedented expansion in output.

The Iron Bridge, built twenty years later, stands today as a monument to this industry and to the faith its promoters had in the value of cast iron as a building material. Even today steel, the successor to cast iron, remains essential to modern manufacturing and construction, a justification of this early faith.

A visit to Ironbridge

Getting there

A visit to Ironbridge is well worthwhile, but because there is so much to see many people stay several days or return a second time (**104**). Ironbridge is well signposted from the M54 and main A routes to Telford, and parking is available at each of the museum sites or on the south side of the Iron Bridge. There are train services to Telford and bus services from Telford town centre. Use the Shropshire Travel Line (Tel. 0345 056785) for information about getting to the area if using public transport.

The Iron Bridge

The Iron Bridge is now in the guardianship of English Heritage and open to the public. On the south side, the Tollhouse contains displays relating to the history of the bridge. The town of Ironbridge has a wide variety of restaurants, pubs and tea rooms, as well as shops catering for visitors. There is a Tourist Information Centre on the Wharfage, just below the Iron Bridge, where details of accommodation, the museums and other sites of interest may be obtained.

The Ironbridge Gorge Museum Trust

Within the Gorge is a group of museums, operated by the Ironbridge Gorge Museum Trust. The Trust is an independent educational charity and relies on money raised by ticket sales to preserve and protect the resources of the valley. A Passport Ticket available at any site provides admission to all the main museum sites and is valid for an indefinite period until each site has been visited once. The museum sites are spread over more than 10 sq. km (4 sq. miles) and so if coming on public transport it is important to check which bus services are

in operation. Museum sites are open seven days a week from 10.00 to 17.00, although some small sites close over winter when it is best to contact the Museum before visiting. The main museum sites are:

Museum of the River and Visitor Centre – located in the Severn Warehouse, the museum houses a 1:200 scale model of the Gorge as it was in 1796 (see **109**), with detailed reconstructions of every house, building and industrial site. Pay and display parking. Leave your car here when walking up to the Iron Bridge.

Museum of Iron, Darby Furnace and Elton Gallery – Abraham Darby I's original furnace can be seen under a cover building (see **101**), while the Great Warehouse now houses displays relating to iron and to Coalbrookdale. The Elton gallery holds a programme of exhibitions each year based on the collection of industrial images and books held by the Museum as well as new material. There is free parking and a coffee shop.

Rosehill House – built soon after 1710 for Richard Ford, then manager of the works, and used by members of the Darby family and their associates, it has been restored as an ironmaster's house of 1848. Parking is available at the Museum of Iron, and there is a tea room.

Blists Hill Open Air Museum – an 18 ha (42 acre) site, which recreates a Shropshire coalfield village in the last few years of the nineteenth century. It is possible to walk along the gaslit streets, past railway sidings, yards and pigsties, shops and offices, hear the hiss of steam and clank of machinery, to taste the butcher's

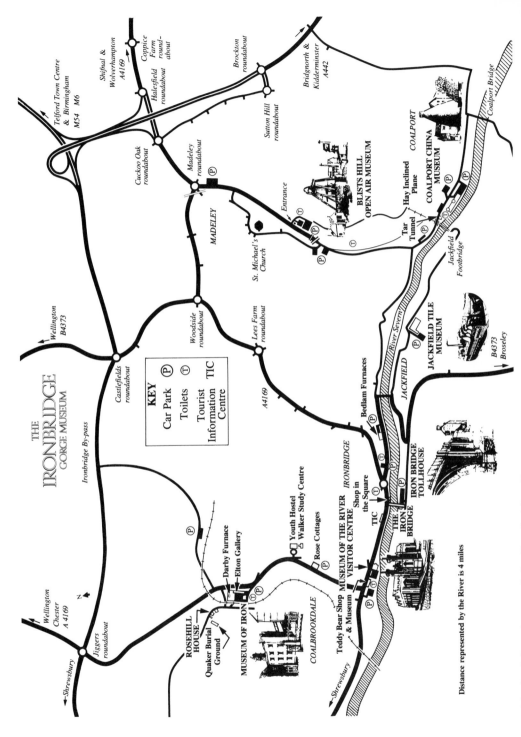

104 *A visitors' map of the Ironbridge Gorge.*

pies and drink beer in the pub. Archaeological monuments which can be seen include the Blists Hill Furnaces, an engine base and coal shafts, a brick and tileworks, the Shropshire Union Canal and the Hay Inclined Plane. A complete working wrought-ironworks has just been reconstructed, with furnaces, a steam hammer, rolling and finishing mills (**105, 106**). This is now the only place in the world to puddle wrought iron. Telephone to check details of operation. Parking is free, and refreshments, hot meals and snacks are available on the site.

Jackfield Tile Museum – the former Craven Dunnill tileworks is now open to the public as a museum of the kaleidoscopic variety of wall and floor tiles produced in the area from the 1850s to 1960s. Above the arch, the old show-room has been restored as it might have been in the nineteenth century (**colour plate 15**) and there is an opportunity to see tiles being manufactured by the Decorative tileworks. Parking is free.

Coalport China Museum – displays of Coalport and Caughley products are housed in the buildings and kilns of the old works; one kiln has been restored and it is possible to see demonstrations of pottery-making skills. The shop carries an extensive range of modern Coalport ware. Free parking.

The Tar Tunnel – near the Coalport China Museum. Begun in 1786 as an underground canal, it produced tar used amongst other things for medicinal purposes. It is possible to walk underground along a section of tunnel, and see the pools of sticky black tar. Free parking nearby, or walk from the Coalport China Museum.

Other archaeological sites
There are also a number of smaller sites and monuments which may be easily visited:

The Quaker Burial Ground (SJ 666050) – just beyond Rosehill house, where many prominent Quakers were interred. Walk up from the Museum of Iron car-park.

105 *The Blists Hill Wrought-Ironworks* (Lance Smith/IGMT).

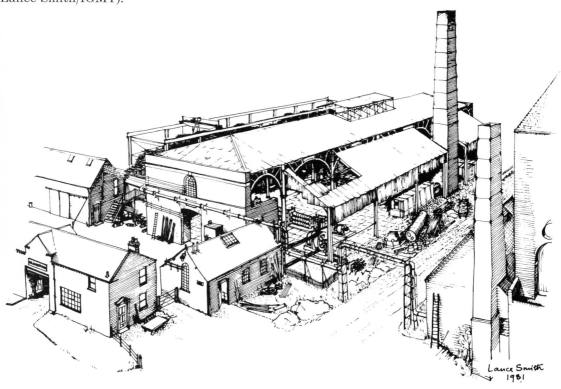

106 *Rolling iron at the Blists Hill Wrought-Ironworks, which now supplies commercial wrought iron* (IGMT).

The Wharfage Limekilns (SJ 668036) – three nineteenth-century limekilns which would have burnt lime from the quarries on Lincoln Hill above. Walk along the Wharfage towards the Iron Bridge from the Museum of the River car-park.

Bedlam Furnaces (SJ 678034) – on the road between Ironbridge and Coalport. Begun in 1757 and made famous by de Loutherburg's painting *Coalbrookdale by Night* (**colour plate 4**). Parking available.

The Hay Inclined Plane (SJ 694026) – may be viewed from within Blists Hill, or from the canalside by the Tar Tunnel. Parking available at the Coalport China Museum.

Coalport Bridge (SJ 702021) – completed in 1818, it is the oldest cast-iron bridge still in use. The ribs beneath the bridge are earlier. It is possible to walk along the riverside past the site of the old inclines.

It is also possible to explore the Gorge on foot. Ironbridge may be approached up the steps from the Square; Benthall Edge and the limestone quarries from the south side of the Iron Bridge. The old railway line provides a convenient link between Coalport and Blists Hill. Maps and information about local walks may be obtained from the Visitor Information Service.

For further information, please contact:
Visitor Information Service
The Ironbridge Gorge Museum
Ironbridge
Telford
Shropshire TF8 7AW.
Tel. (0952) 433522 (weekdays)
    (0952) 432166 (weekends)
 Fax. (0952) 432204.

People

Abraham Darby I (1678–1717) A Quaker iron-master who first smelted iron with coke at Coalbrookdale in 1709. He moved in 1708 from Bristol, where he was apprenticed to a maker of malt mills and had set up a brass foundry, to Coalbrookdale where he leased an ironworks, intending to make brass. He successfully smelted iron with coke and used the iron for casting pots and other goods. He built Dale House overlooking the works for himself shortly before his death.

Abraham Darby II (1711–1763) The son of Abraham Darby I, he took over the Coalbrook-dale works in 1728. He was responsible for installing an engine to circulate water at Coalbrookdale, and more importantly for developing a way of making pig iron with coke which could be converted into wrought iron. He adopted railways to supply the works, and integrated different aspects of the company's operations.

Abraham Darby III (1750–1789) He entered the works in 1768 with his brother Samuel and managed the works during a period when the concern became the largest ironworks in Britain. He took a leading role in the construction of the Iron Bridge.

Abraham Darby IV (1804–1878) He entered the works in the late 1820s, and with his brother Alfred undertook major rationalization of the works. The first Darby to move away from Quakerism, he was also responsible for the display of ornate art castings at the Great Exhibition of 1851.

107 *William Reynolds* (1974.207).

Richard Reynolds (1735–1816) A member of a Bristol Quaker family, who moved to Shropshire in 1756. He married Hannah, daughter of Abraham Darby II. He managed the works after the latter's death and was involved in the expansion of the works, the use of the first iron rails and experiments with making wrought iron.

William Reynolds (1758–1803) The most versatile of the Shropshire ironmasters (**107**). He was a partner in the company until 1796 when the Darby/Reynolds partnership dissolved. Thereafter he was a partner in the Madeley Wood and Ketley ironworks. His business interests included china manufacturing at Coalport, alkali working at Wombridge, glass-making at Wrockwardine Wood, limestone working and the development of a new town at Coalport. His personal interests included the study of chemistry, botany, geology and mineralogy and he associated with such men as Earl Dundonald, Erasmus Darwin and Thomas Telford.

John Wilkinson (1728–1808) 'Iron Mad' Wilkinson, as he was nicknamed, was perhaps the greatest ironmaster of the late eighteenth century (**108**). He owned iron furnaces at Willey, Hollinswood, Hadley and Snedshill in Shropshire, Bersham and Brymbo in Denbighshire and Bradley in Staffordshire. He delighted in finding new uses for iron and collaborated with Abraham Darby III in building the Iron Bridge. He also built the first iron boat in 1787 and even made himself an iron coffin. He led an eccentric and scandalous life. On his death, his heirs, legitimate and illegitimate, spent most of his vast fortune in litigation.

108 *John Wilkinson* (IGMT).

109 *Model of the Gorge on August 11, 1796 –
the day of the visit of the Prince and Princess
of Orange. Now housed in the Museum of the
River* (Michael Worthington).

Further reading

General Works

Cossons, N., 1987, *The BP Book of Industrial Archaeology,* 2nd ed., Newton Abbott, David and Charles.

Trinder, B.S., 1981, *The Industrial Revolution in Shropshire*, 2nd ed., Chichester, Phillimore.

Trinder, B.S., 1988, *The Most Extraordinary District in the World,* 2nd ed., Chichester, Phillimore.

Victoria History of the Counties of England, 1908, *Shropshire: Volume 1,* (repr. 1968) London, Oxford University Press for the Institute of Historical Research.
- 1985, *Shropshire: Volume 11*, London, Oxford University Press for the Institute of Historical Research.
- (forthcoming), *Shropshire: Volume 10.*

Detailed coverage of the archaeology of the area can be found in a series of reports published by the Ironbridge Institute and available from the Ironbridge Gorge Museum. These include the four interim reports of the Nuffield Archaeological Survey by Catherine Clark and Judith Alfrey, and the series produced by the Ironbridge Gorge Museum Archaeology Unit, edited by Michael Trueman.

Medieval Origins

Pannet, D.J., 1981, 'Fish Weirs of the River Severn', in *The Evolution of Marshland Landscapes*, Oxford, Oxford University Department for External Studies.

Victoria History of the Counties of England, 1973, *Shropshire: Volume 2,* London, Oxford University Press for the Institute of Historical Research.

Wanklyn, M., 1969, 'John Weld of Willey: estate management 1631–1660', *West Midlands Studies* 4, 63–71.

Wiggins, W.E., 1986, *Ancient Woodland in the Telford Area*, Telford, Telford Development Corporation.

Coal: foundation of industry

Brown, I., 1976, *The Mines of Shropshire,* Buxton: Moorland.

Cox, N., 1990, 'Imagination and innovation of an industrial pioneer: the first Abraham Darby', *Industrial Archaeology Review*, 12,2, 127–44.

Nef, J.U., 1932, *The Rise of the British Coal Industry*, London, Routledge.

Prestwich, J., 1835, 'On the geology of Coalbrookdale', *Transactions of the Geological Society of London*, Series 2, 5.3:413–95.

Trinder, B.S. and Cox, J., 1980, *Yeomen and Colliers in Telford*, Chichester, Phillimore.

Iron

Mott, R.A., 1957–8, 'Abraham Darby I and II and the coke-iron industry', *Transactions of the Newcomen Society* 31, 49–94.

Raistrick, A., 1989, *Dynasty of Ironfounders*, 2nd ed., London, Longmans, Green & Co.

Trinder, B.S., 1978, *The Darbys of Coalbrookdale*, revised edition, Chichester, Phillimore.

Tylecote, R., 1976, *A History of Metallurgy*, London, The Metals Society.

Wanklyn, M., 1982, 'Industrial development in the Ironbridge Gorge before Abraham Darby', *West Midlands Studies*, 15, 3–7.

Pottery

Benthall, E., 1955, 'Some 18th century Shrop-

135

shire potteries', *Transactions of the Shropshire Archaeological Society*, 55, 159–70.

Draper, J., 1984, *Post Medieval Pottery 1650–1800*, Princes Risborough, Shire.

Edmundson, R.S., 1979, 'Coalport China Works: a comparative study of the premises and the background to their development', *Industrial Archaeology Review, 3,2: 122–45.*

Godden, G.A., 1969, *Caughley and Worcester Porcelains 1775–1800*, London.

Houghton, A.W.J., 1968, 'Caughley porcelain works near Broseley, Salop', *Industrial Archaeology*, 5, 186–92.

Jewett, L., 1878, *Ceramic art of Great Britain*, London, Virtue.

Malam, J., 1981, 'White salt-glazed stoneware manufacture at Jackfield, *West Midlands Archaeology*, 24, 45–50.

Randall, J., 1877, *Clay industries... on the banks of the Severn*, Madeley, Salopian and West Midland Office.

Bricks

Dawes, N.M.K., 1979, *A history of brick and tile production on the Coalbrookdale Coalfield*, Mss. IGMT library.

Hammond, M., 1981, *Bricks and Brickmaking*, Princes Risborough, Shire Publications.

Mugridge, A.J., 1987, *Brick and roofing tile manufactories in the Severn Gorge,* Jackfield, Orchard Press.

Limestone

Brown, I.J. and Adams, D.R., 1967, *A history of limestone mining in Shropshire*, Special Account No. 6, Shropshire Caving and Mining Club.

Brown, I.J., 1979, 'Underground in the Ironbridge Gorge', *Industrial Archaeology Review*, 3,2, 158–69.

Murchison, R.I., 1867, *Siluria,* 4th ed., London, John Murray.

Ove Arup, 1986, *Limestone mines in the Wrekin area,* Shrewsbury, Shropshire County Council.

Toghill, P., 1990, *Geology in Shropshire,* Shrewsbury, Swan Hill Press.

The Iron Bridge

Cossons, N. and Trinder, B.S., 1979, *The Iron Bridge: Symbol of the Industrial Revolution*, Bradford-on-Avon, Moonraker Press.

Smith, S., 1979, *A view from the Iron Bridge*, Ironbridge, Ironbridge Gorge Museum Trust.

Transport

Lewis, M.J.T., 1974, *Early Wooden Railways*, London, Routledge.

Trinder, B.S., 1992 (2nd ed.), *Coalport New Town*, Ironbridge, Ironbridge Gorge Museum Trust.

Victorian Ironbridge

Herbert, A.T., 1979, 'Jackfield decorative tiles in use', *Industrial Archaeology Review*, 3,2: 146–52.

Muter, W.G., 1979, *The Buildings of an Industrial Community: Coalbrookdale and Ironbridge*, Chichester, Phillimore.

The admiration of strangers

Cossons, N., 1979, 'Ironbridge – the first ten years', *Industrial Archaeology Review* 3,2: 179–86.

Raistrick, A., 1990, *Dynasty of Ironfounders,* 2nd ed., York, Sessions (with final chapter on the last 30 years).

Glossary

adit Mine dug horizontally into a mineral seam. Also known as an insett or drift mine.

assart A medieval term for land cleared for cultivation from the waste or forest.

bell pit A pit sunk into a shallow coal seam. Coal was then worked from around the base. Bell pits are characterized by a circular ring of spoil thrown up around the top of the shaft. The name derives from the shape of the pit when viewed in section.

blast furnace A vertical structure in which ironstone, coke or charcoal and a flux are burnt to produce molten iron, using a blast of air to aid the process. Invented in Belgium by c.1400 AD, the blast furnace spread through Britain in the sixteenth and seventeenth centuries.

bloomery A small charcoal-fired hearth for the production of wrought iron direct from the ore.

bottle kiln A kiln in which pottery was fired. The name comes from the bottle-shaped outer structure which protected the actual kiln in the centre.

brewhouse A small building adjoining or to the rear of a house, used for the messier household tasks such as brewing beer, butchering pigs or laundry. Usually equipped with a cold bench or settle, and often a large heated cauldron. Common at a time when most cooking and eating was done on a range in the parlour which also doubled as a sitting room.

burgage plot Long thin strips of land laid out in a medieval town, and let on a yearly rent.

Clod Coal Seam of coal found in the Coal Measures which was low in sulphur. Once coked, it provided an ideal fuel for iron smelting, one which was as close in composition to charcoal as possible.

coke Coal burned in conditions starved of oxygen in order to drive off impurities.

earthenware Slightly porous pottery, usually glazed.

encaustic tile Decorative floor tile with impressed pattern infilled with clay of a different colour. Introduced into Britain from the Low Countries in the thirteenth century and used extensively as a church paving. Manufacturing was revived in the mid-nineteenth century in response to the demands of church restoration and the use of tiles was made popular by architects such as Pugin. Manufacturers such as Mintons, Craven Dunnill and Maw & Co. began making such tiles, but soon expanded the repertoire of techniques to include coloured glazes, mosaics, different forms of printing and decoration.

forge A place where wrought iron is shaped by hammering or pressing it

foundry A place where iron is re-melted, and cast into objects.

hay Medieval enclosure or park often used for keeping deer.

inclined plane Sloping trackway with rails up which goods could be raised or lowered on waggons. At the top was a winding drum to hold the cable, powered either by a steam engine or by gravity, using the weight of the descending car to lift the other. The seventeenth-century 'tylting rails' would have been an early version.

lime kiln A kiln in which limestone is burnt with charcoal or coal to produce lime (calcium oxide). Lime can be used as fertilizer or in building as mortar or limewash. The kiln is tall and lined with bricks with a firehole or 'eye' at the bottom where the fire is lit, and through which the burnt lime is drawn off. Lime kilns occur singly, in pairs or in banks of multiple kilns.

long wall mining System of mining whereby a continuous face of coal about 91m (300ft) long is worked. As the coal is taken away, leftover stone is packed into drystone walls to support the roof. It was developed in the seventeenth century and known as the 'Shropshire' method.

pig iron (or **cast iron**) Hard, brittle iron produced in a blast furnace. The iron contains many impurities. The molten iron runs out of the furnace into channels with small off-shoots, reminiscent of a sow and piglets.

plateway A railway line consisting of L-shaped cast-iron plates on which ran waggons with iron wheels. Invented by John Curr, and introduced here in the 1790s to replace the earlier iron rails without flanges, it was in use by the Coalbrookdale Company by 1767. The earlier iron rails were modelled on, and in fact replaced, wooden rails.

porcelain A white translucent pottery made from china clays, ball clay, feldspar and flint and fired at high temperatures. Developed in China, the first porcelain was brought to Europe in the twelfth century. There was a great seventeenth-century vogue for Chinese porcelains, and manufacturers in first Germany and later Britain tried to copy it. Caughley produced a soft-paste porcelain, which required two firings.

probate inventory A list of possessions compiled at the death of a person as part of the process of administering their estate, and drawn up by an 'honest and skilful' person. Probate inventories are available for this area between about 1613 and 1750.

pug mill A device for breaking up clay. Early versions consisted of a barrel containing knives, usually turned by a horse. Later pug mills used a metal screw and were powered by steam or electricity.

saggar A rough clay vessel, used to protect a finer pot from damage during firing. Salt-glaze saggars usually have holes in the sides to allow the salt vapour to reach the pot inside.

semi-plastic process A brick- and tile-making process introduced in the 1890s. The clay contained less moisture than previously; extrusion machines were used to mould bricks and tiles.

slag Glassy material created in a blast furnace, when impurities in the metal fuse and float to the top. Slag from a cold blast furnace is often blue/grey in colour.

smelting The process in which a metallic ore is changed into metal using heat and chemical energy.

tithe map A parish map prepared as part of the process of converting annual church tithes, traditionally paid in corn, to a cash sum. These often provide the first large-scale maps of an area, and are accompanied by an apportionment listing owners, occupiers, land-use and areas. They must be treated with care, as industrial features are often not shown as they were not titheable. Usually produced soon after the 1836 Tithe Commutation Bill.

trow One of the many types of boat used on the river Severn for transporting goods until the mid-nineteenth century. Equipped with sails, but often bow-hauled by men or later horses. Upper Severn trows carried from 40 to 80 tons and were about 18m (60ft) long, smaller than the sea-going vessels which plied the Lower Severn.

tub boat A small flat-bottomed boat about 6m (20ft) long and 2m (6ft 4in) broad used on canals to transport goods. Usually pulled by horses.

turnpike road A road on which gates or barriers were erected for the collection of tolls, which would then be used to maintain the road.

waggonway A term for an early railway line, often used interchangeably with railway or tramway. Used here to refer to a wooden railway on which horse-drawn waggons were used; introduced by 1608 and used until replaced by iron rails in 1767.

wrought iron Pure, fibrous form of iron, which can be shaped by hammering. Produced directly by heating iron in a charcoal fire from ancient times. After the introduction of the blast furnace, wrought iron was produced as a secondary process.

Index

(Page numbers in **bold** refer to illustrations)